Adult Coloring Book
Animal Designs

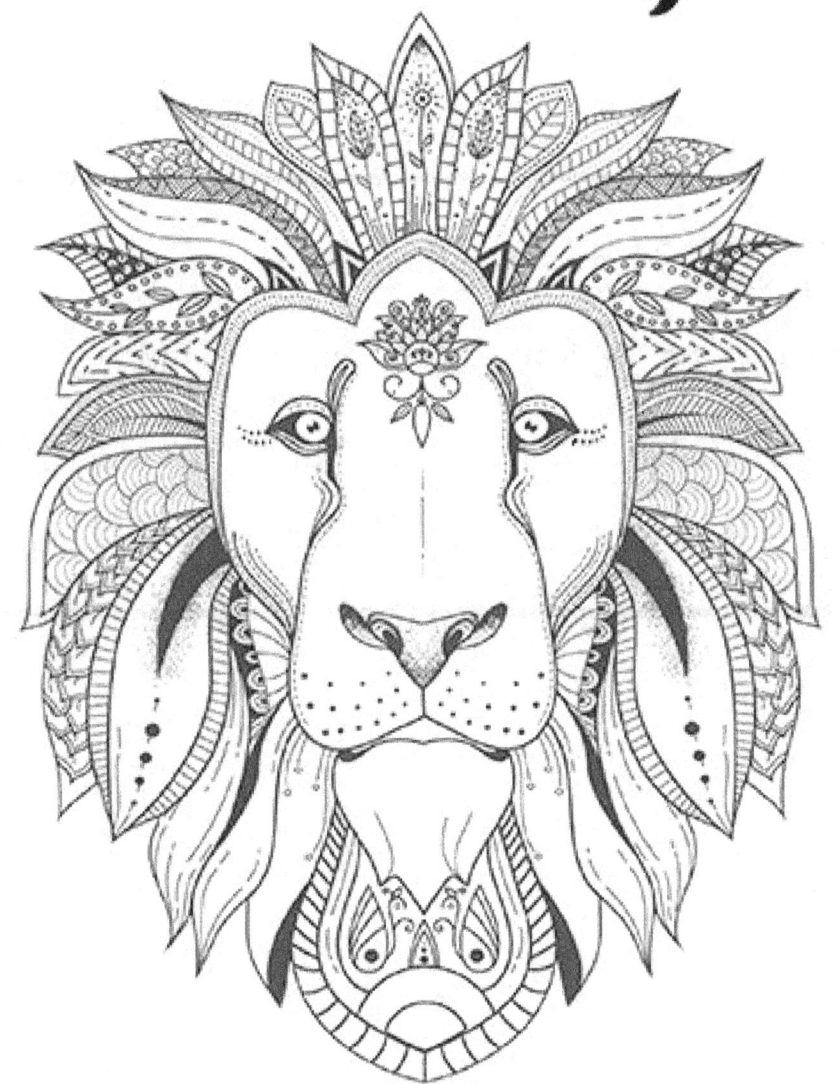

by creative thinking

Copyright © 2021 by Creative Thinking

All Rights Reserved. No Part Of This Publication May Be Reproduced, Distributed, Or Transmitted In Any Form Or By Any Means, Including Photocopying, Recording, Or Other Electronic OR Mechanical Methods.

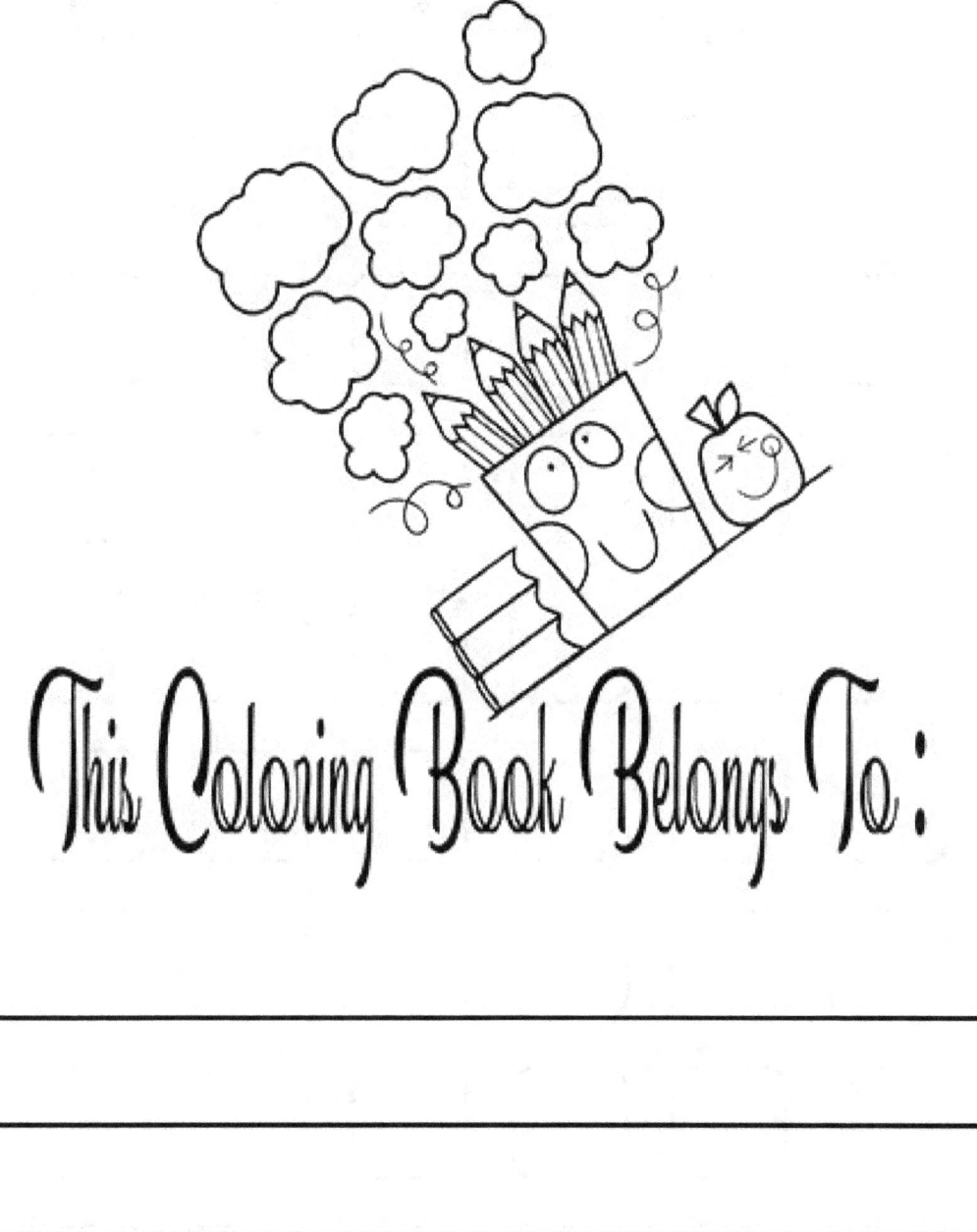

This Coloring Book Belongs To:

_____

_____

_____

_____

Colour Test Page

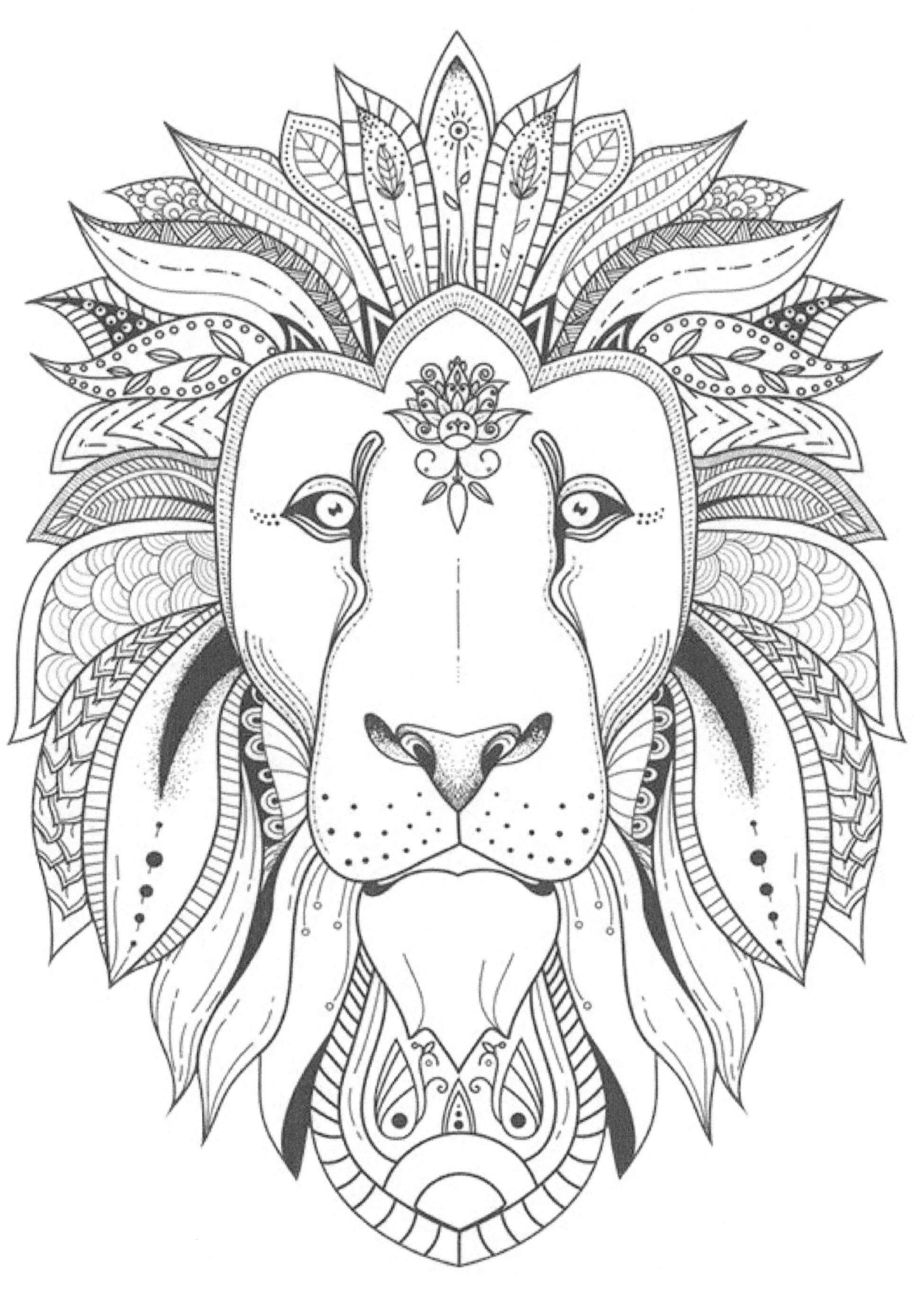

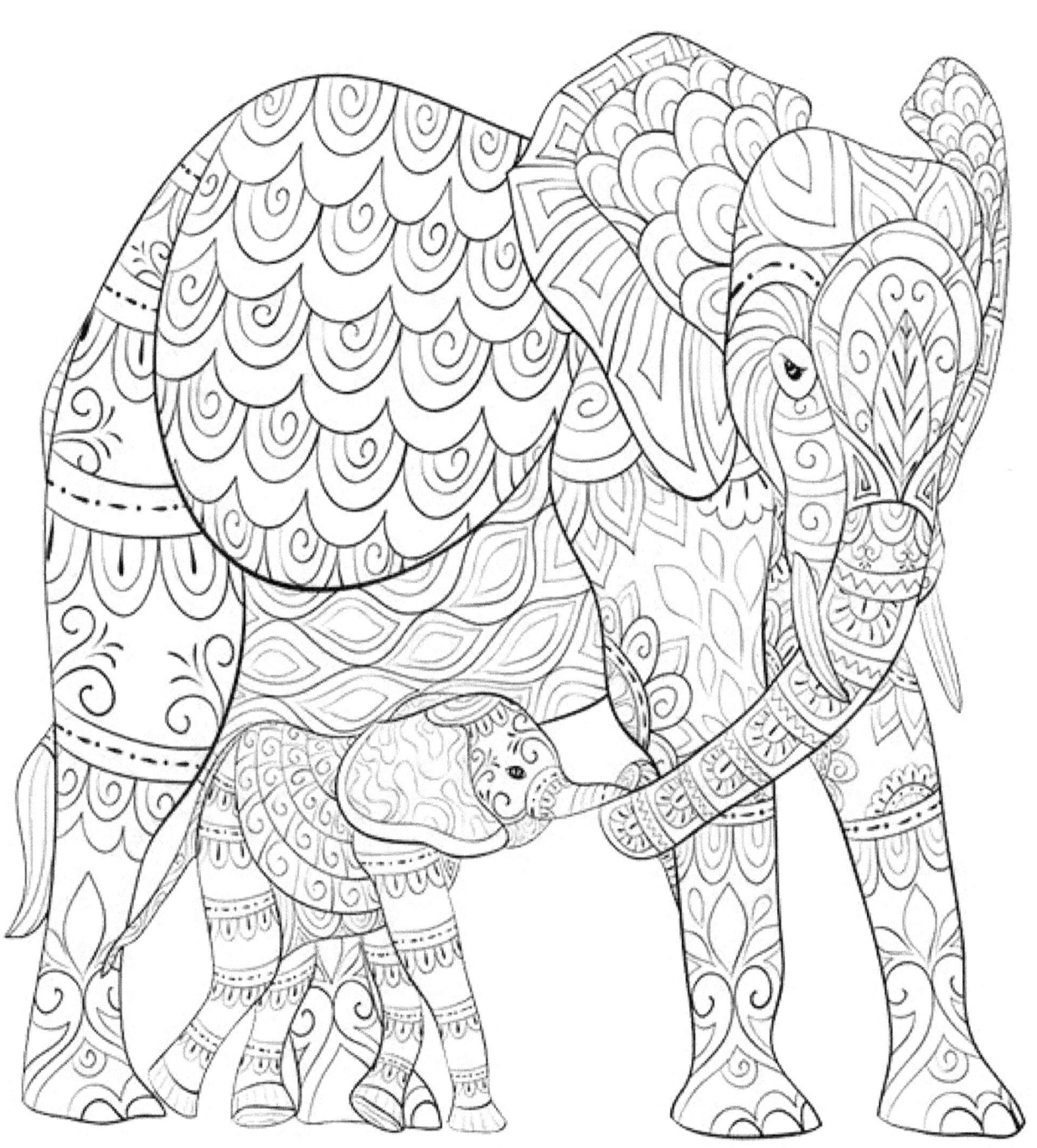

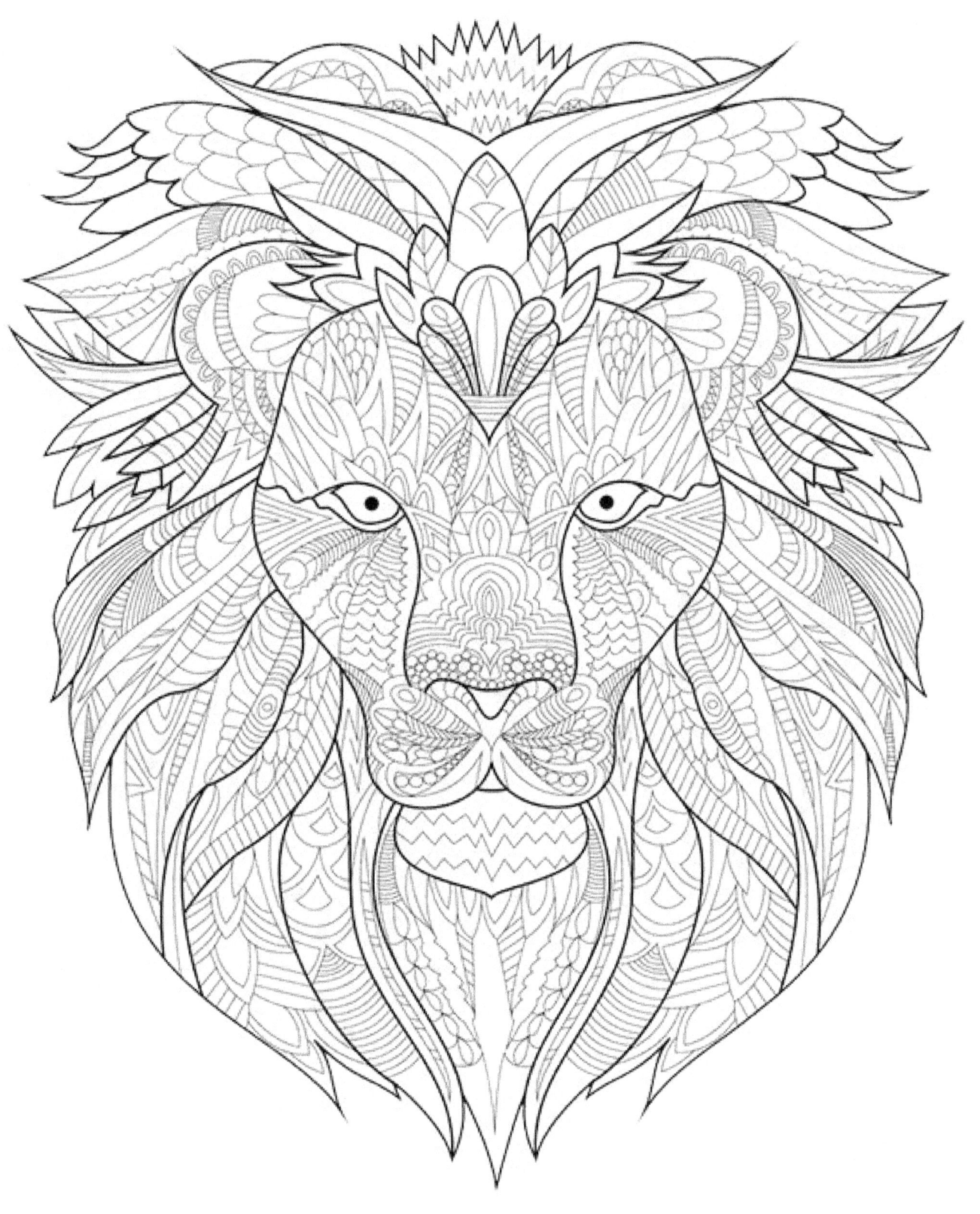

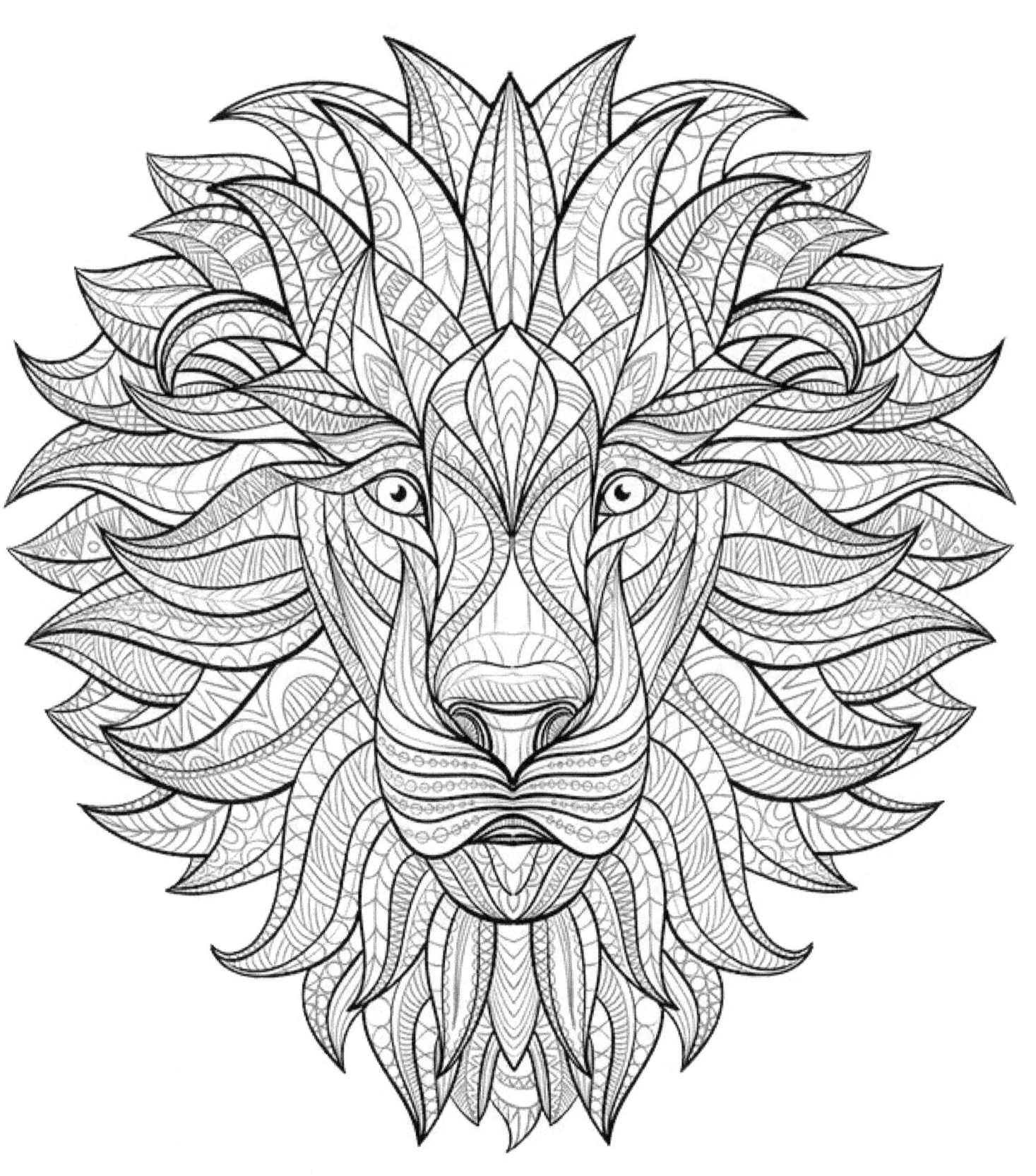

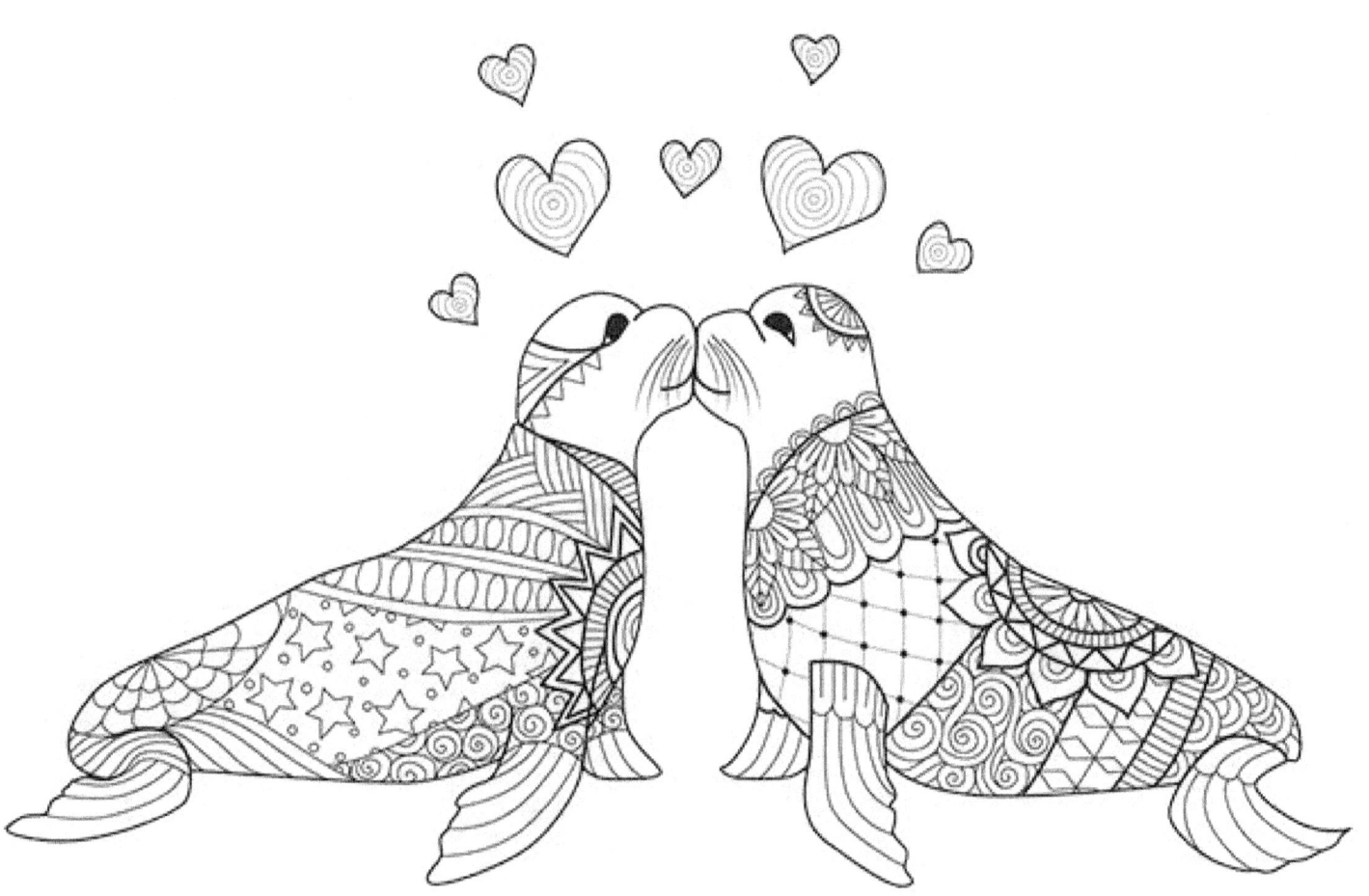

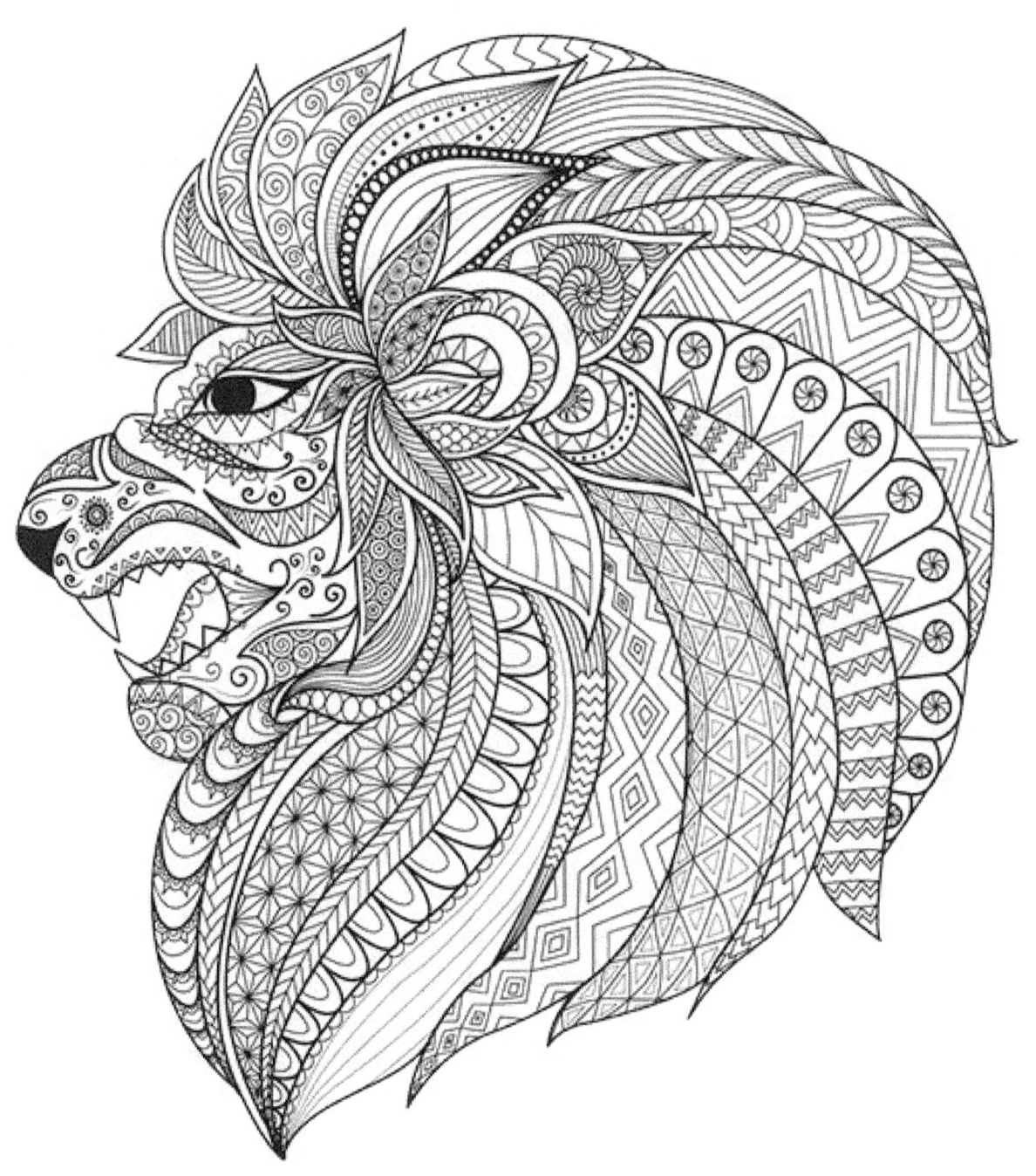

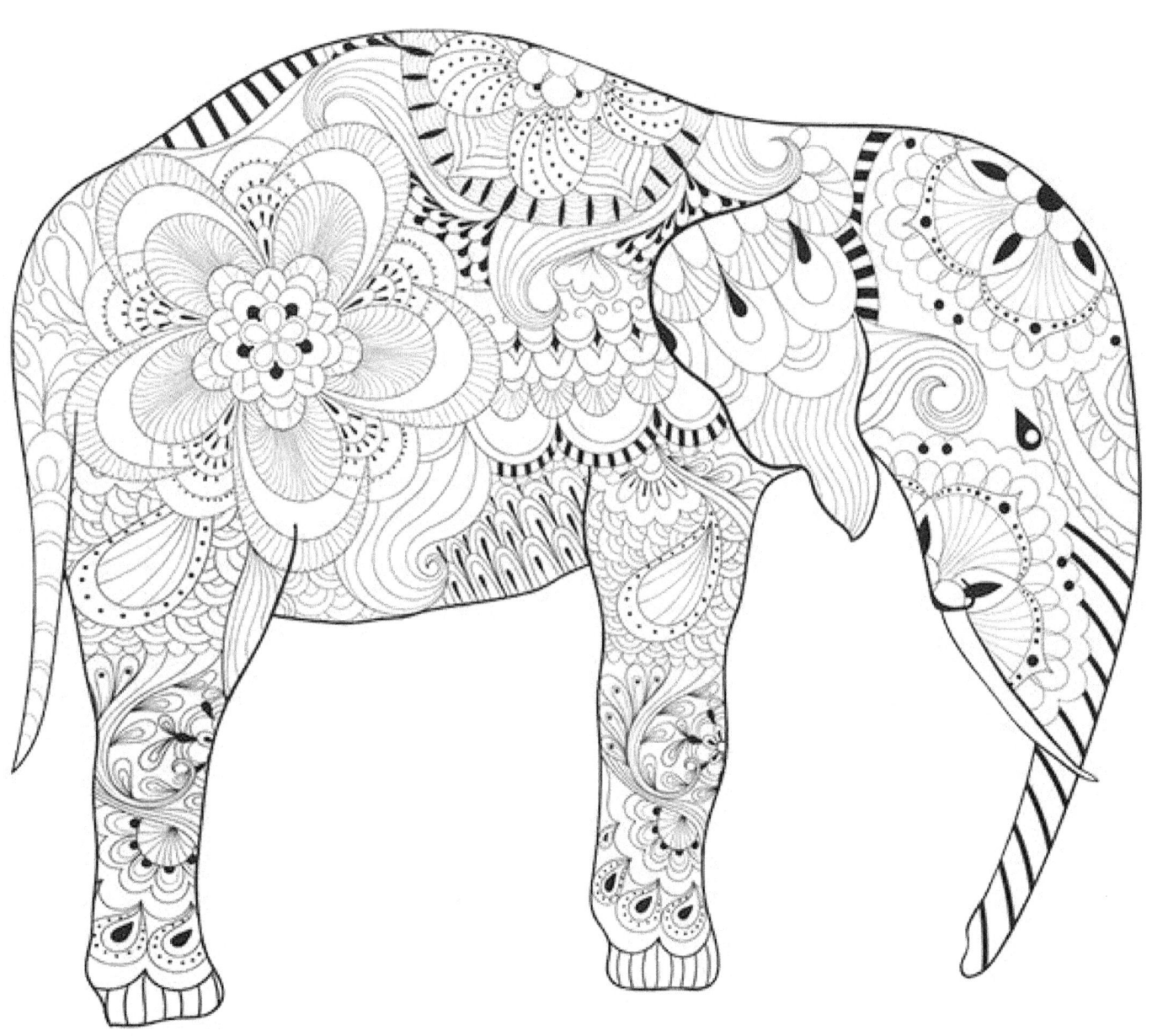

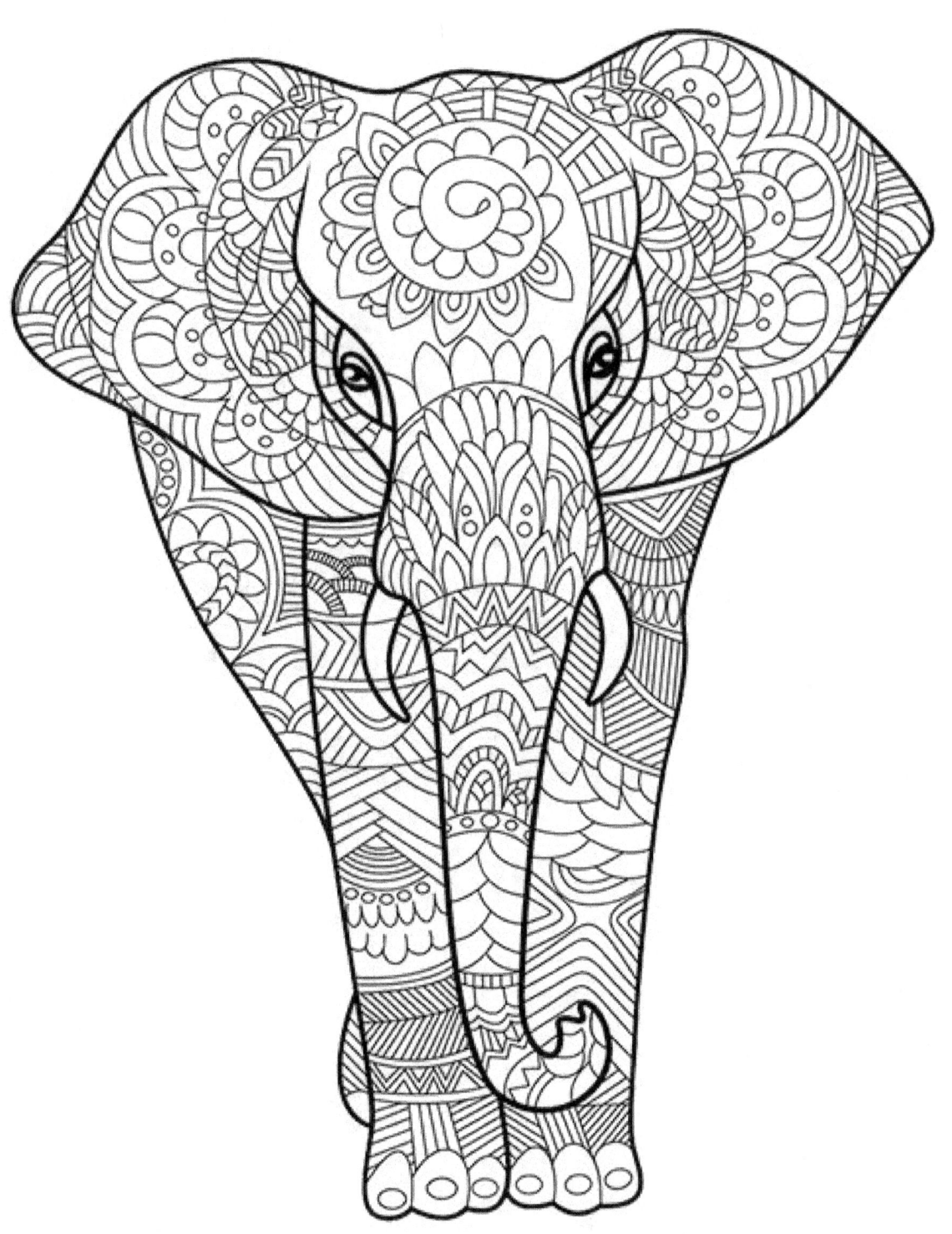

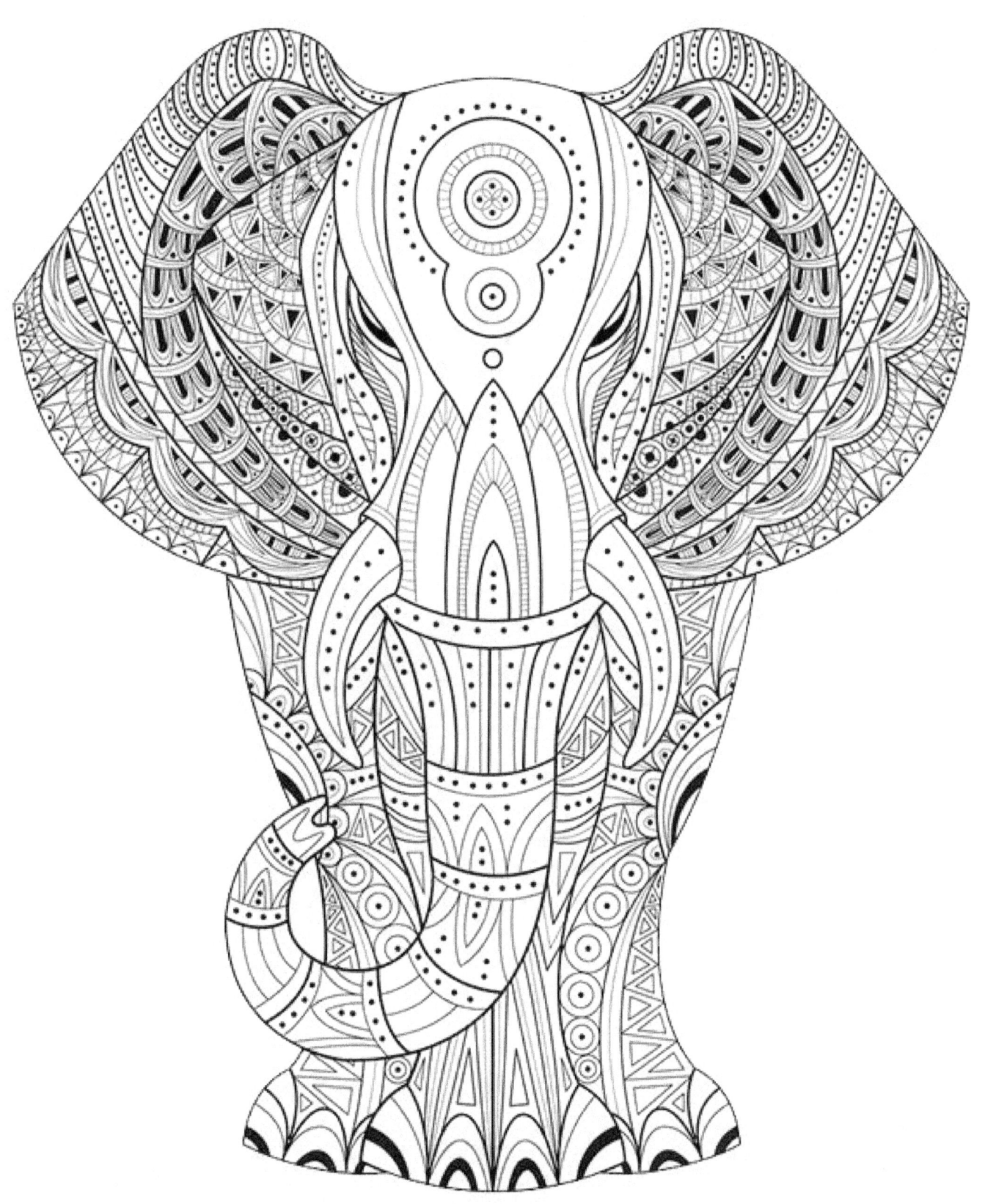

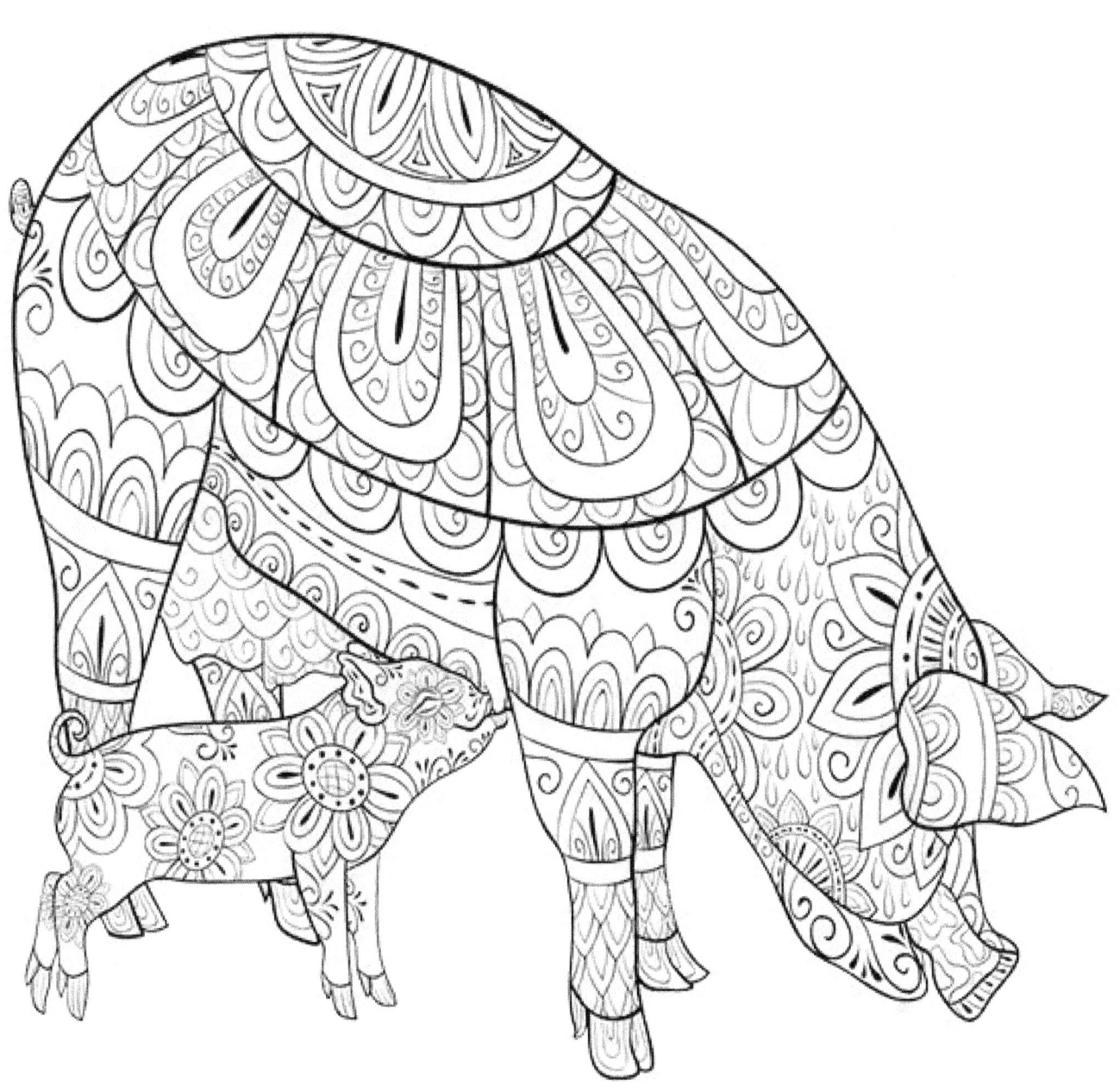

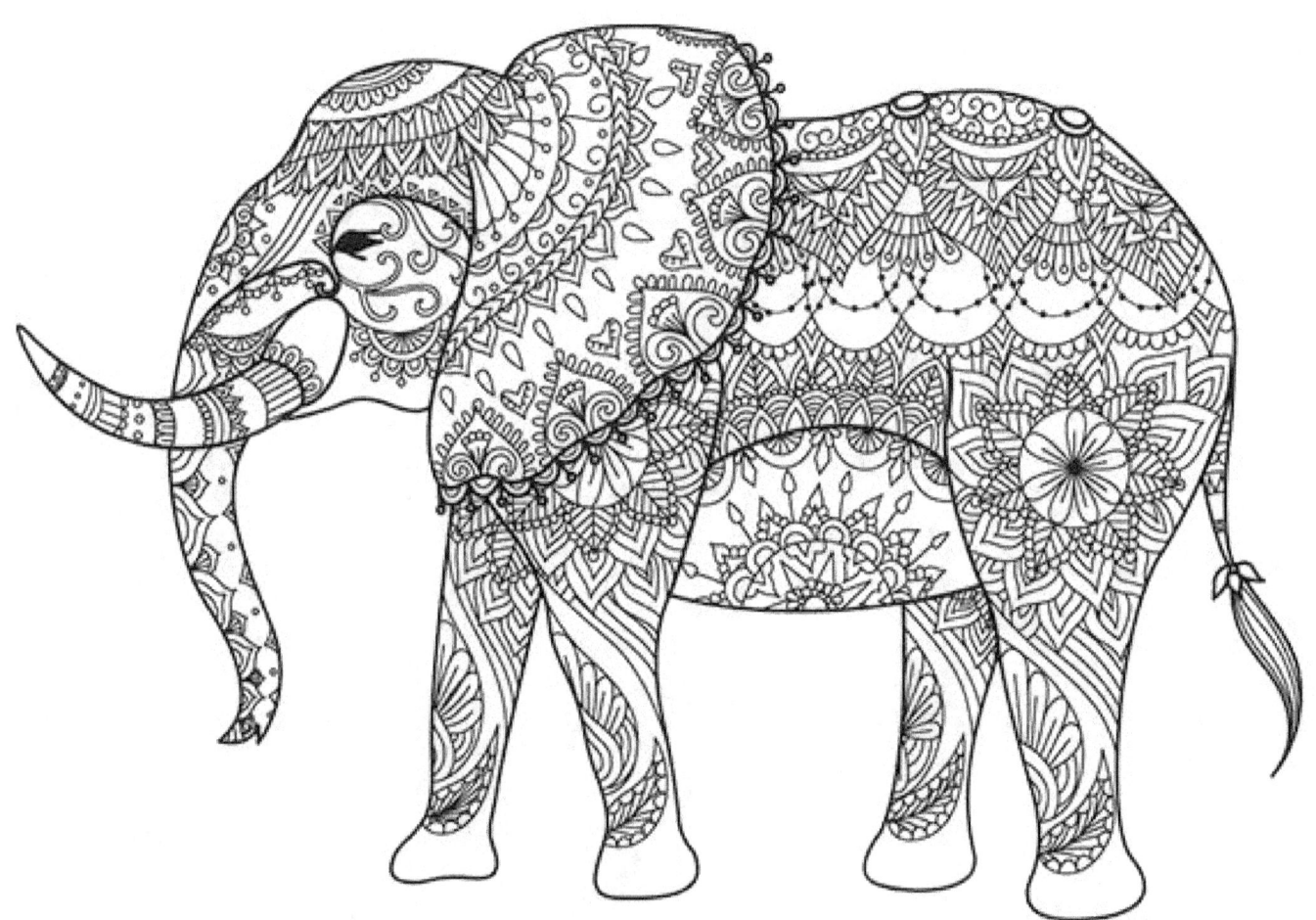

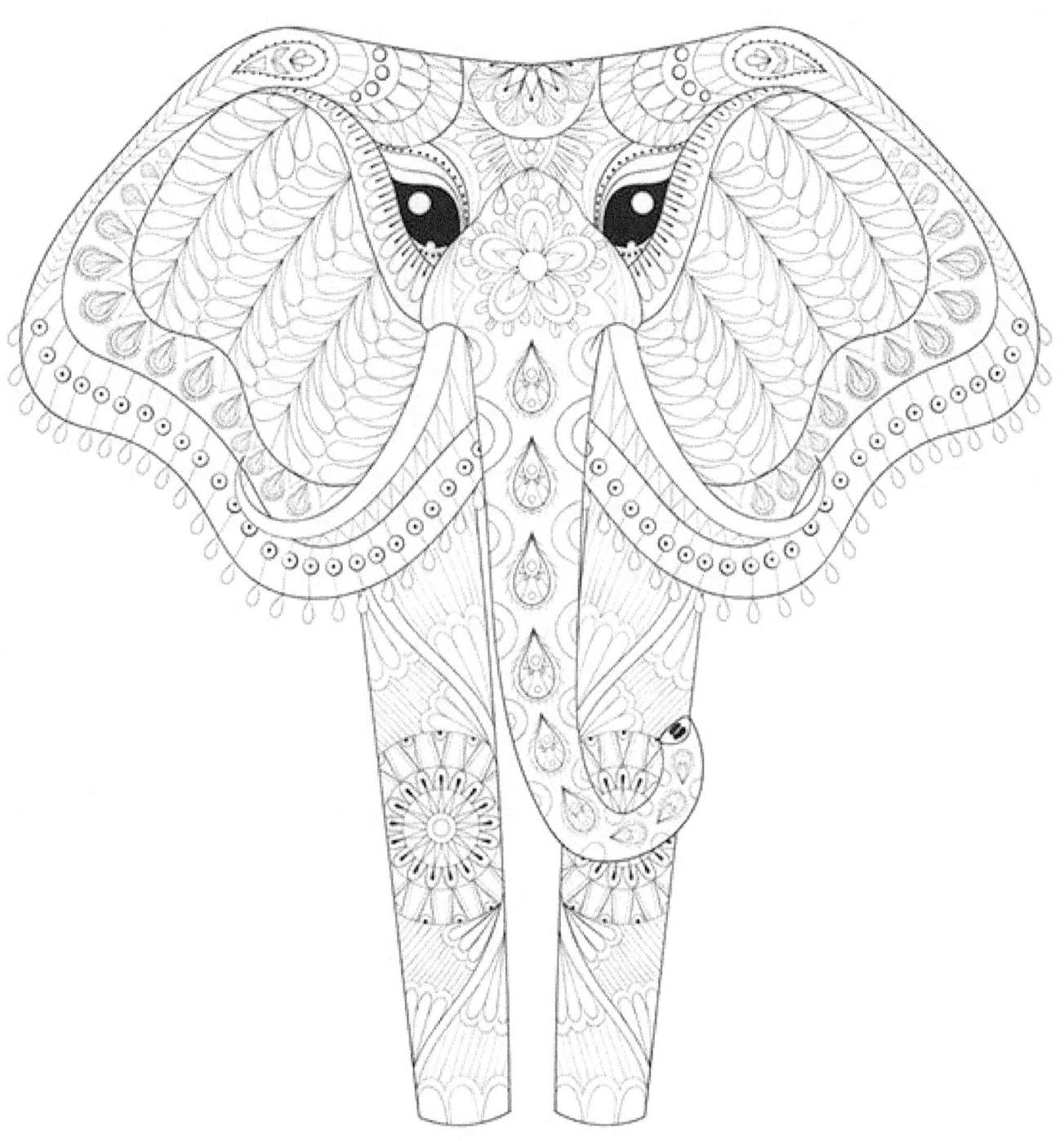

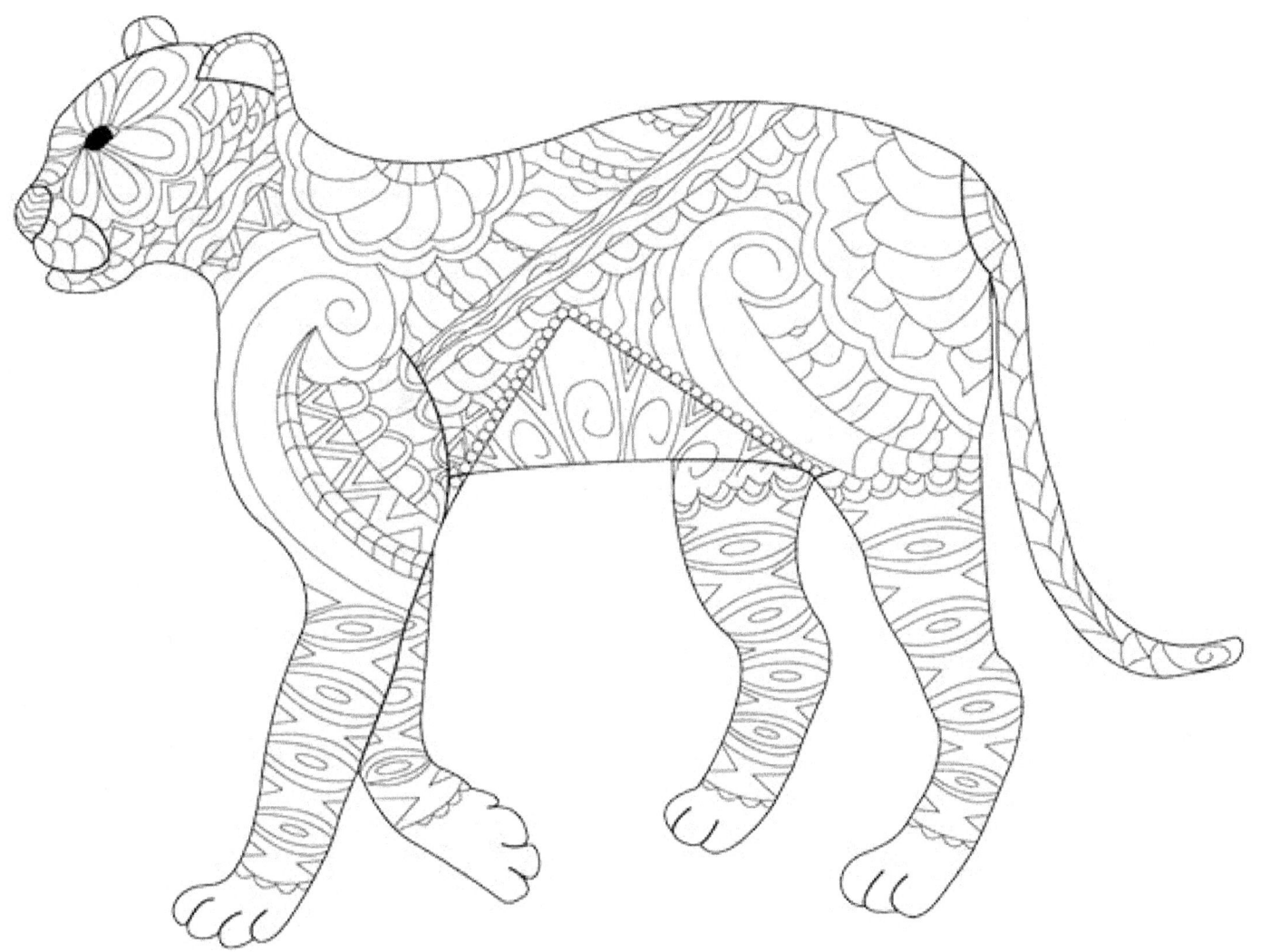

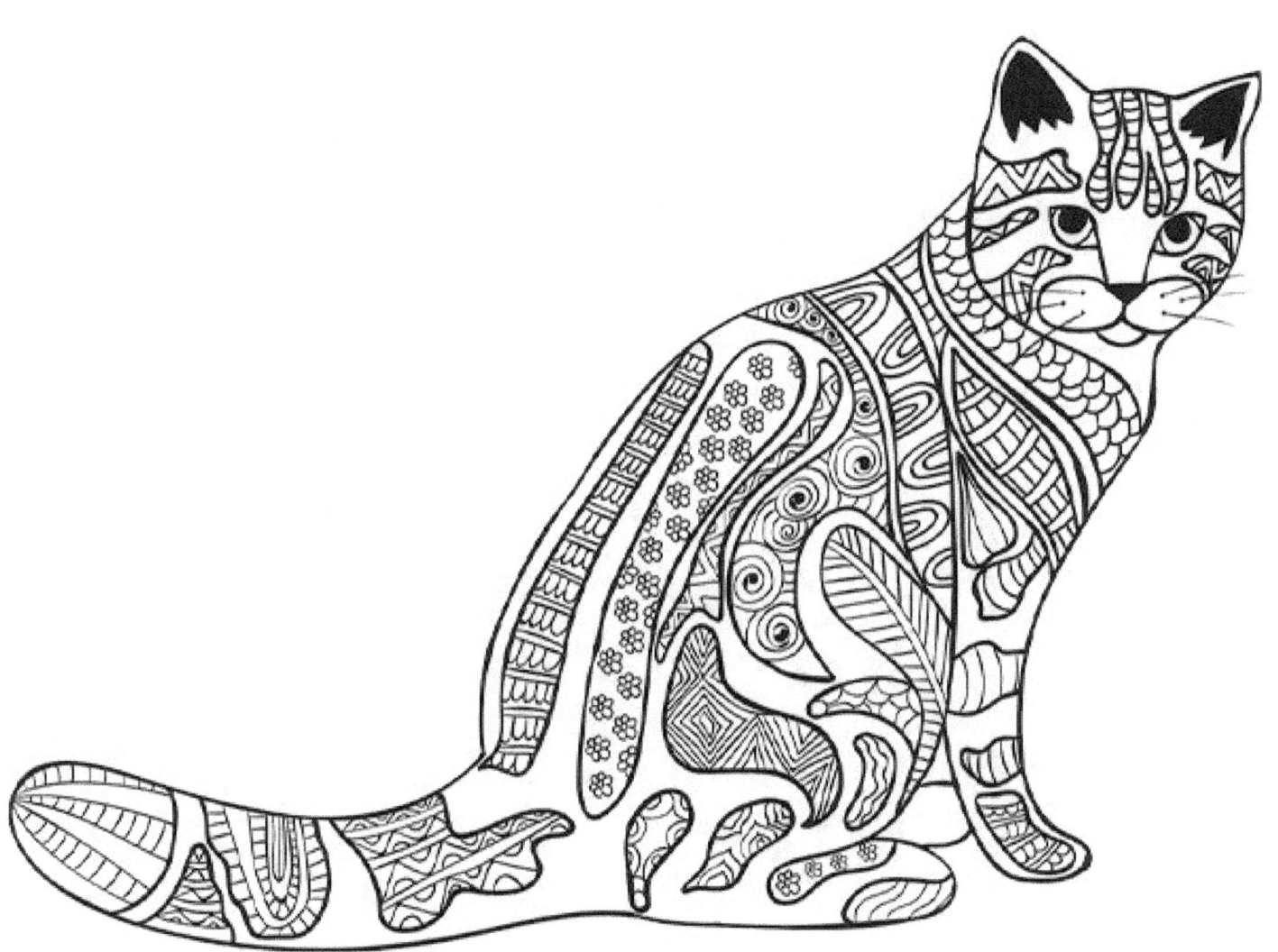

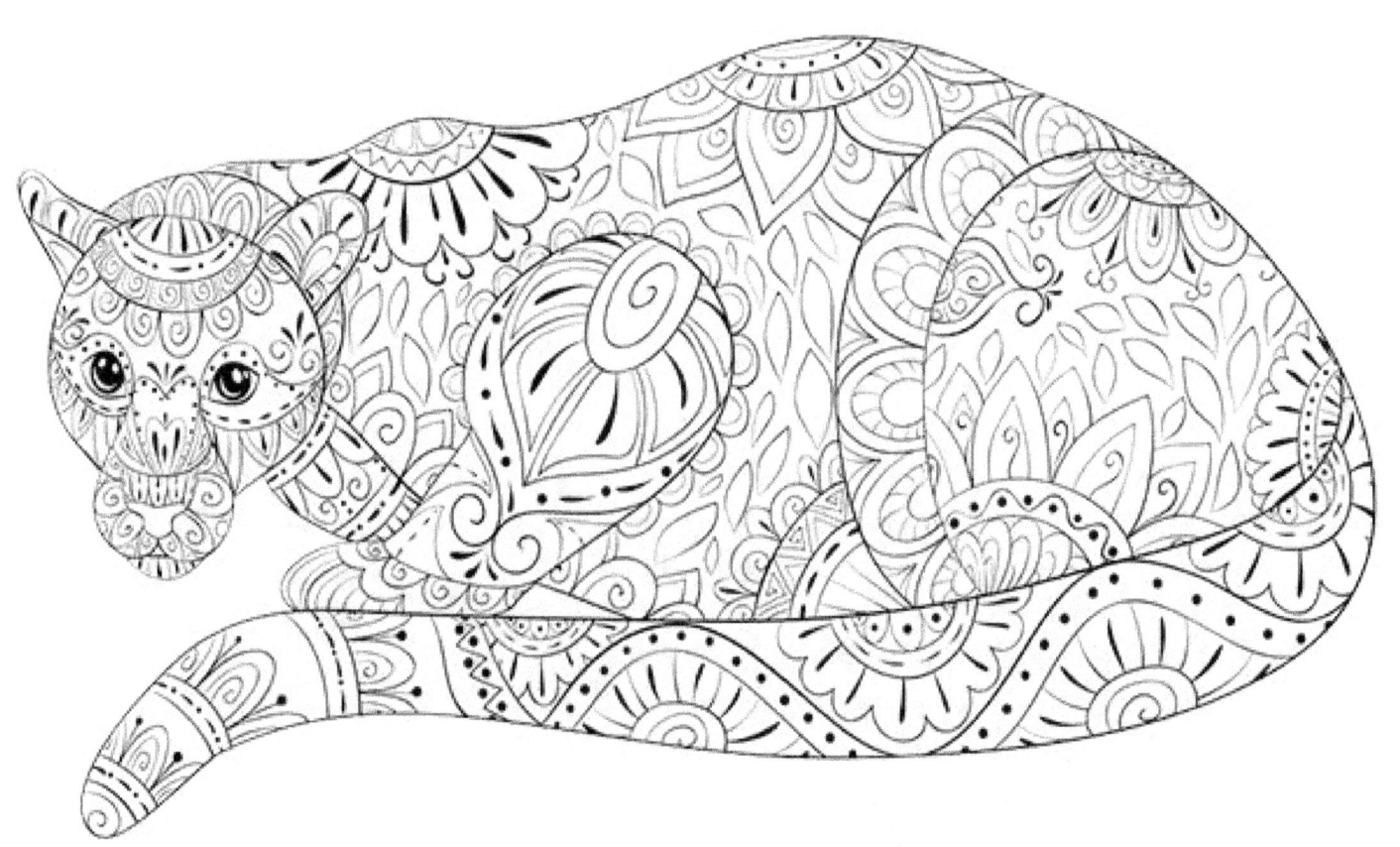

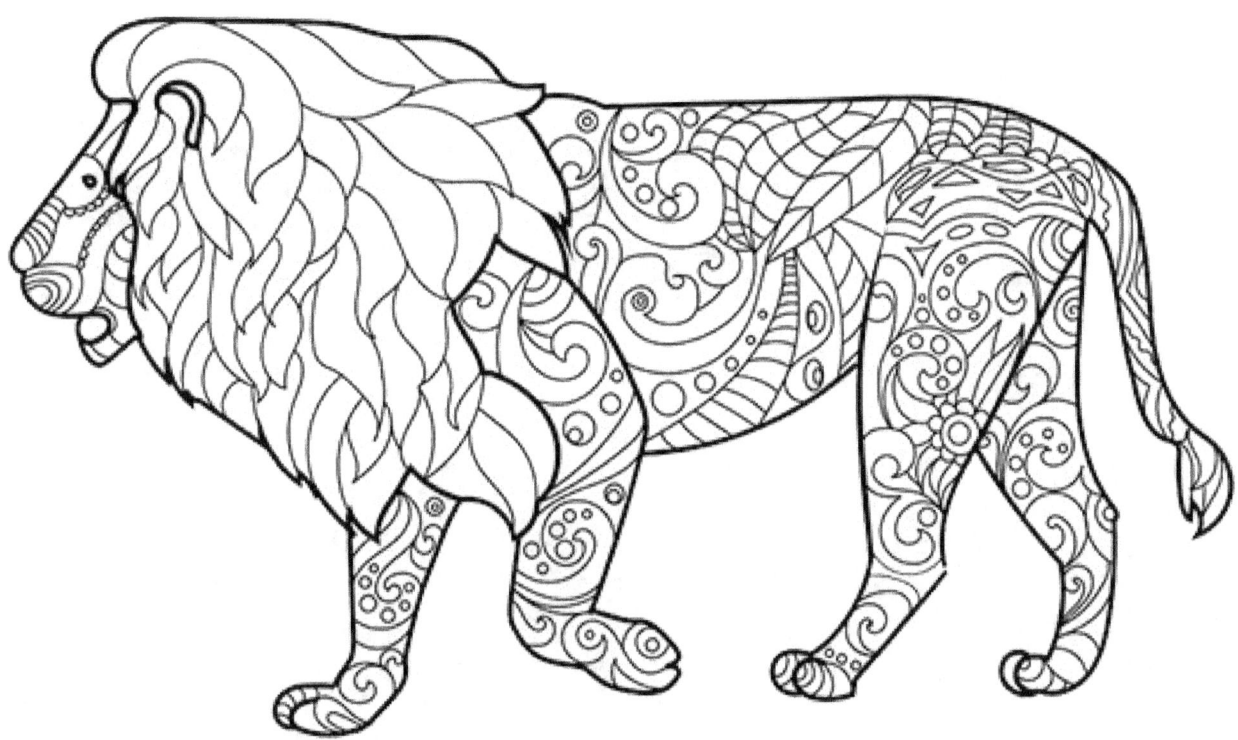

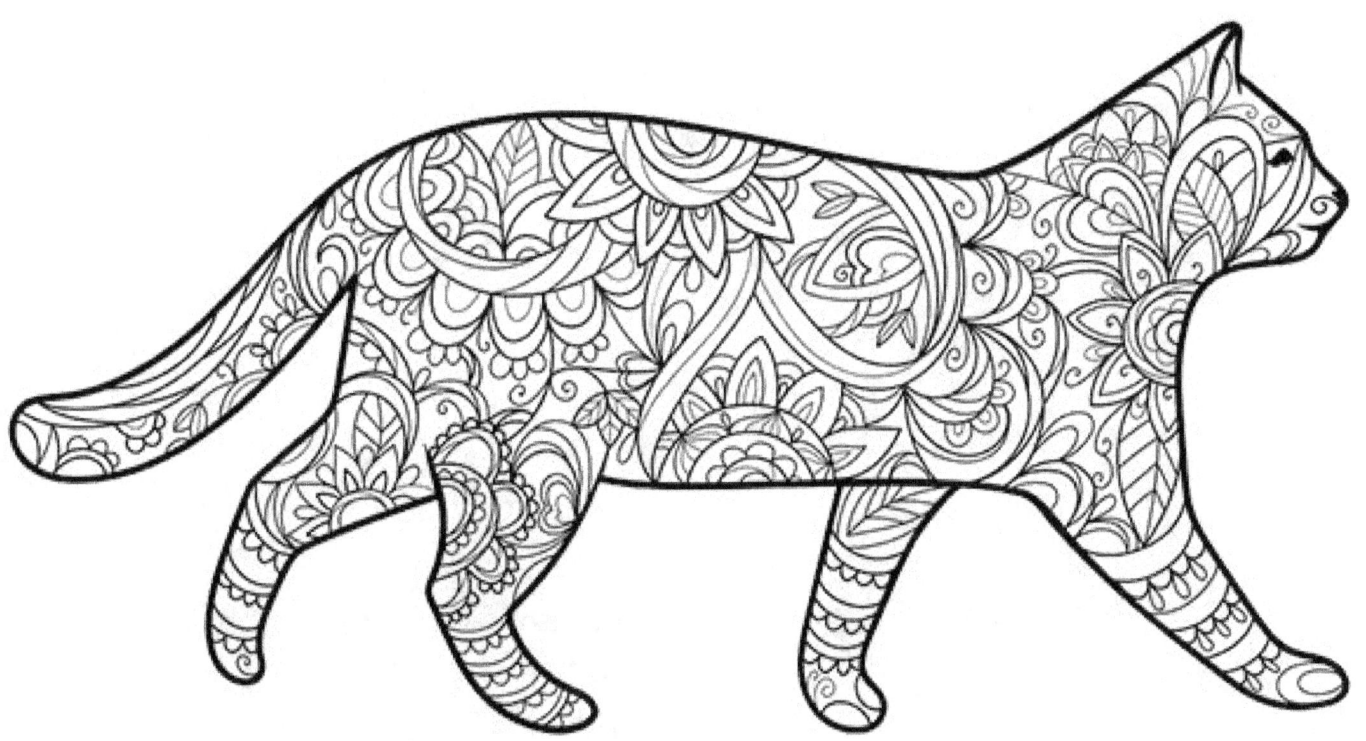

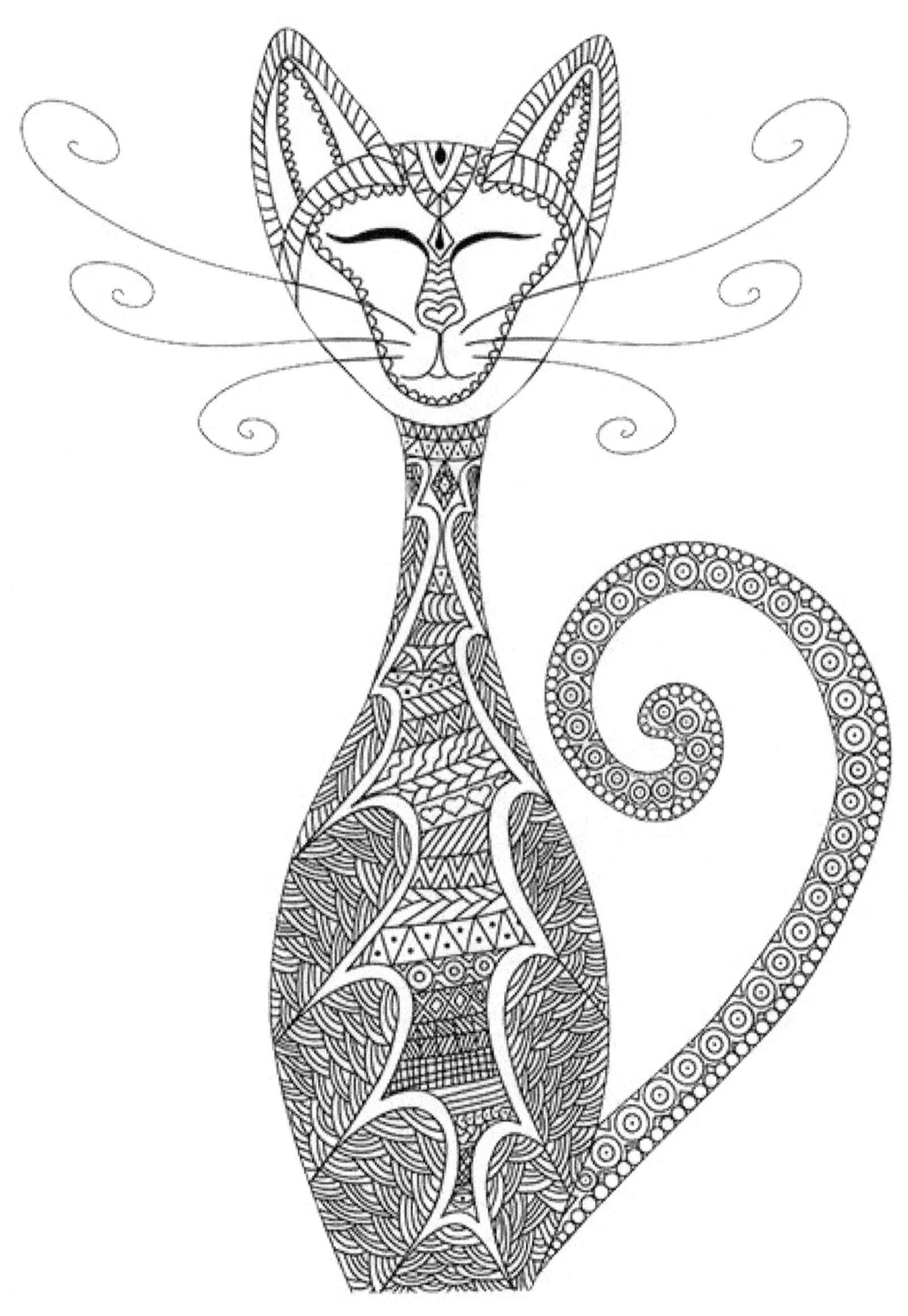

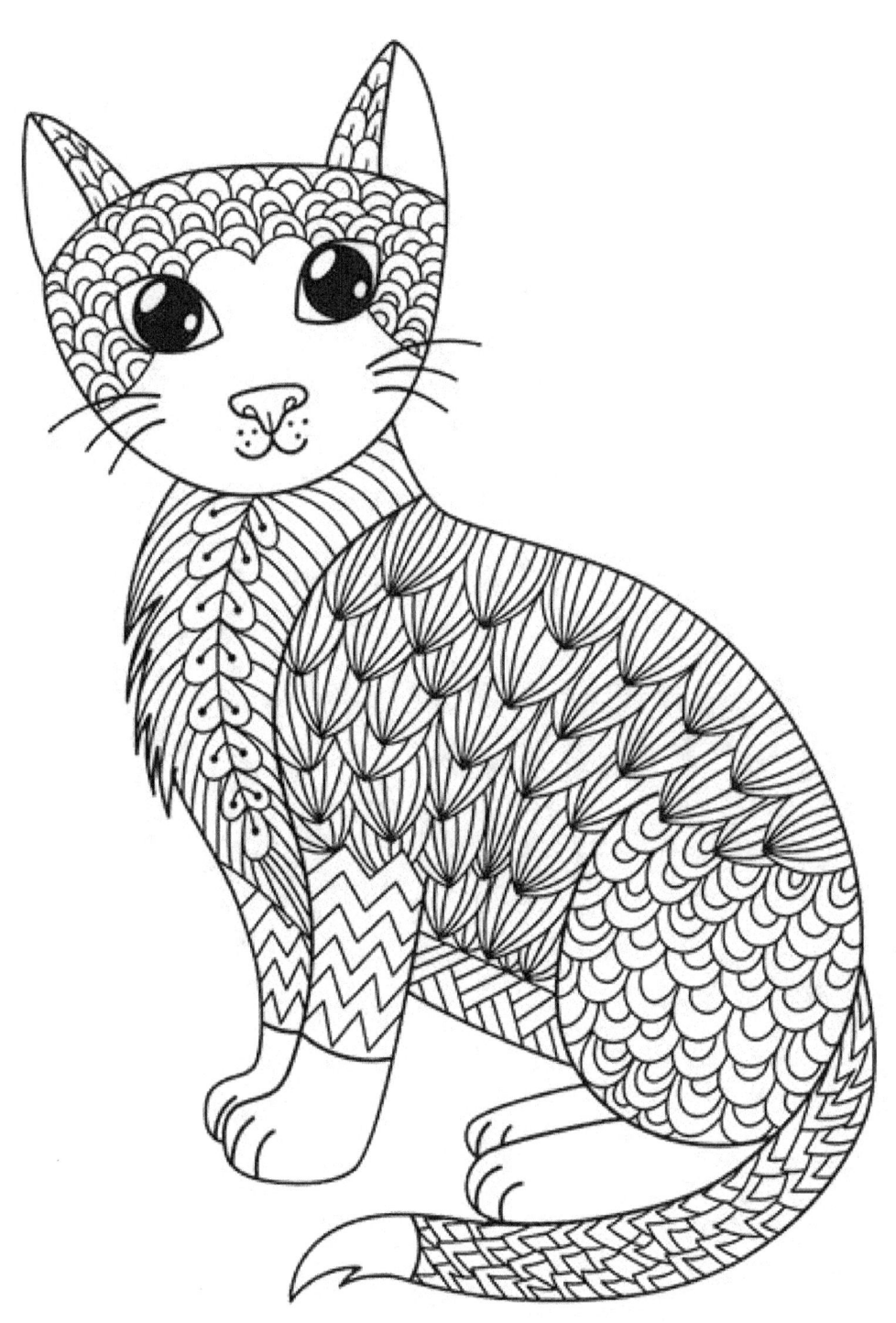

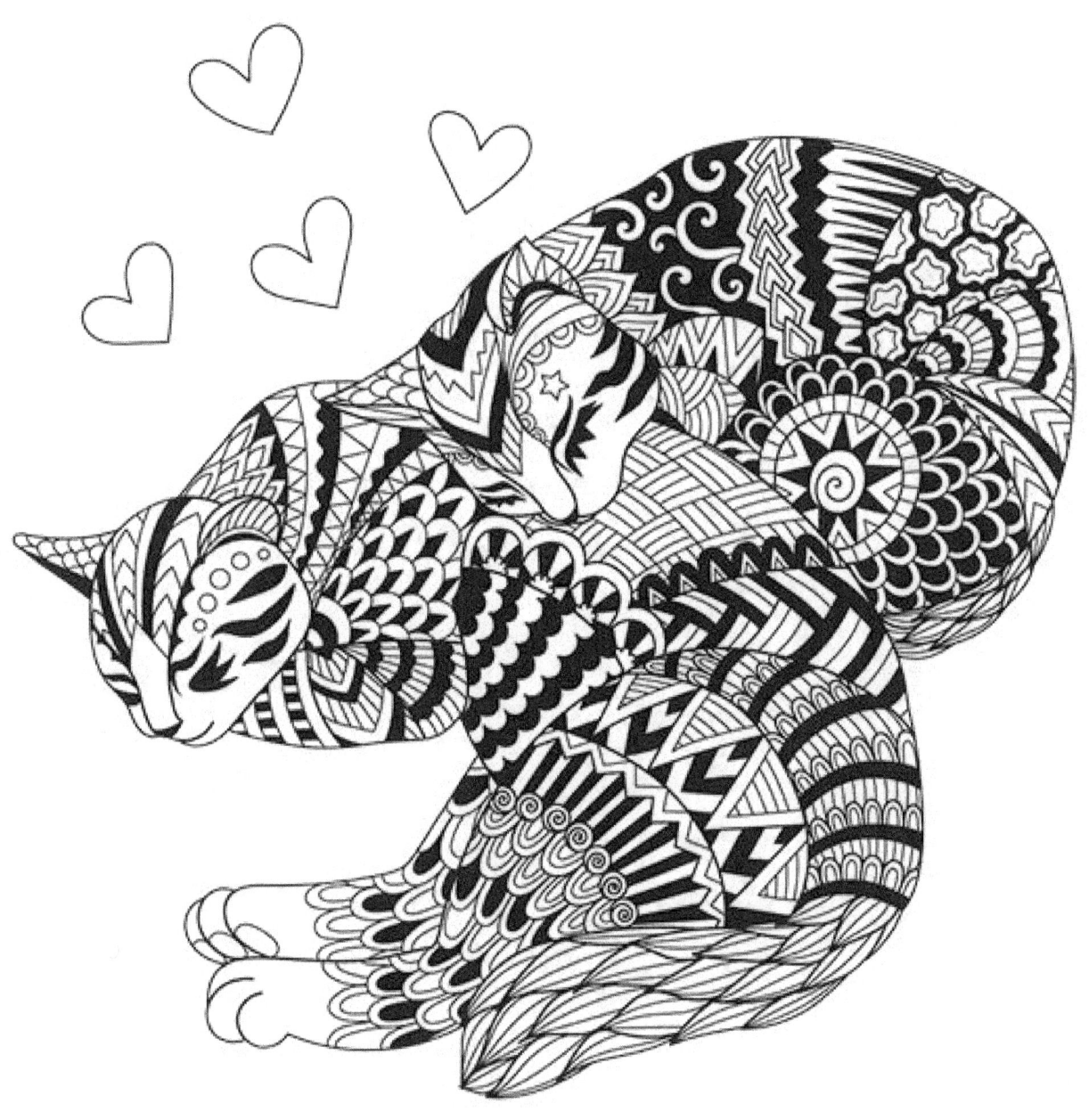

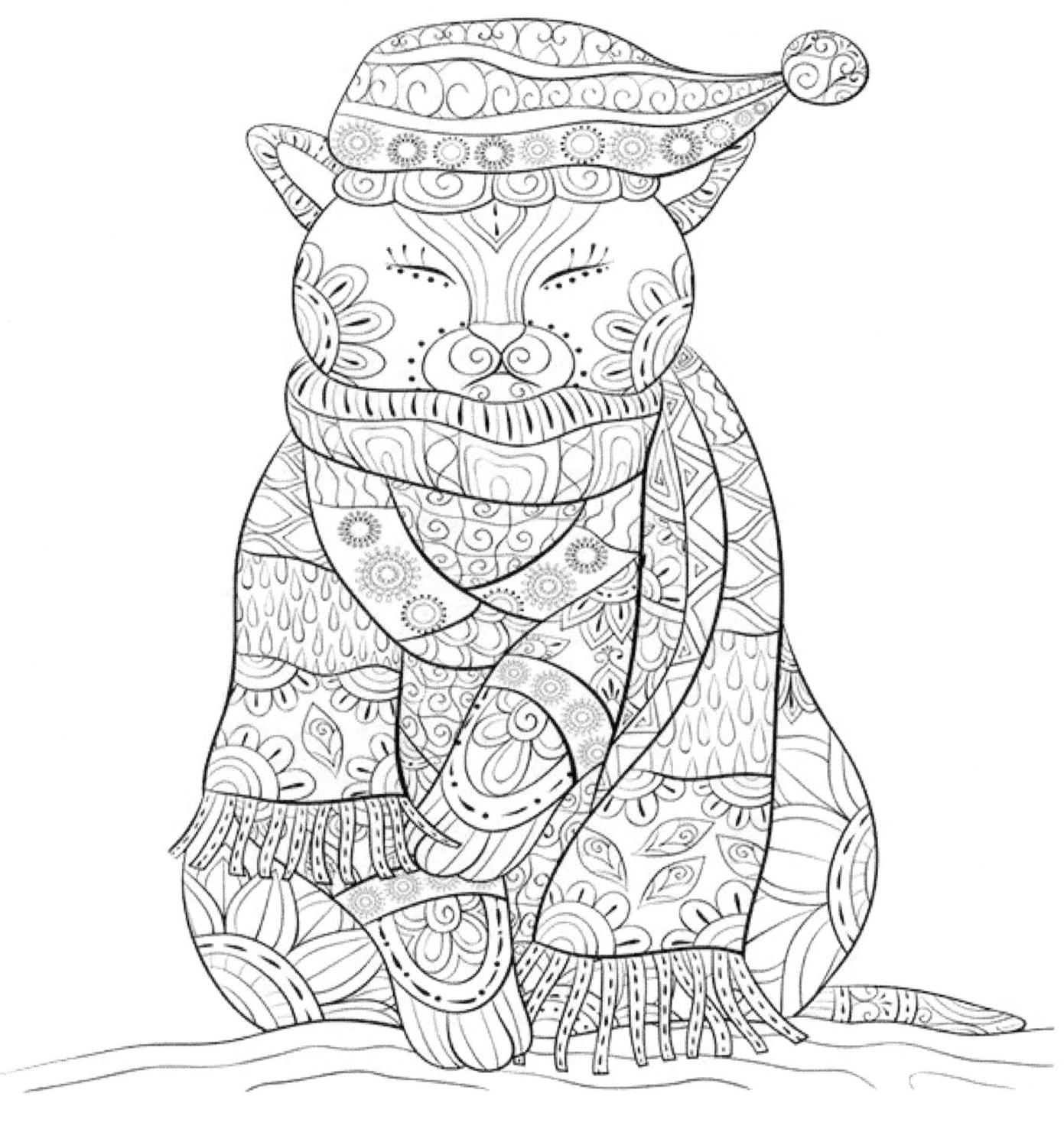

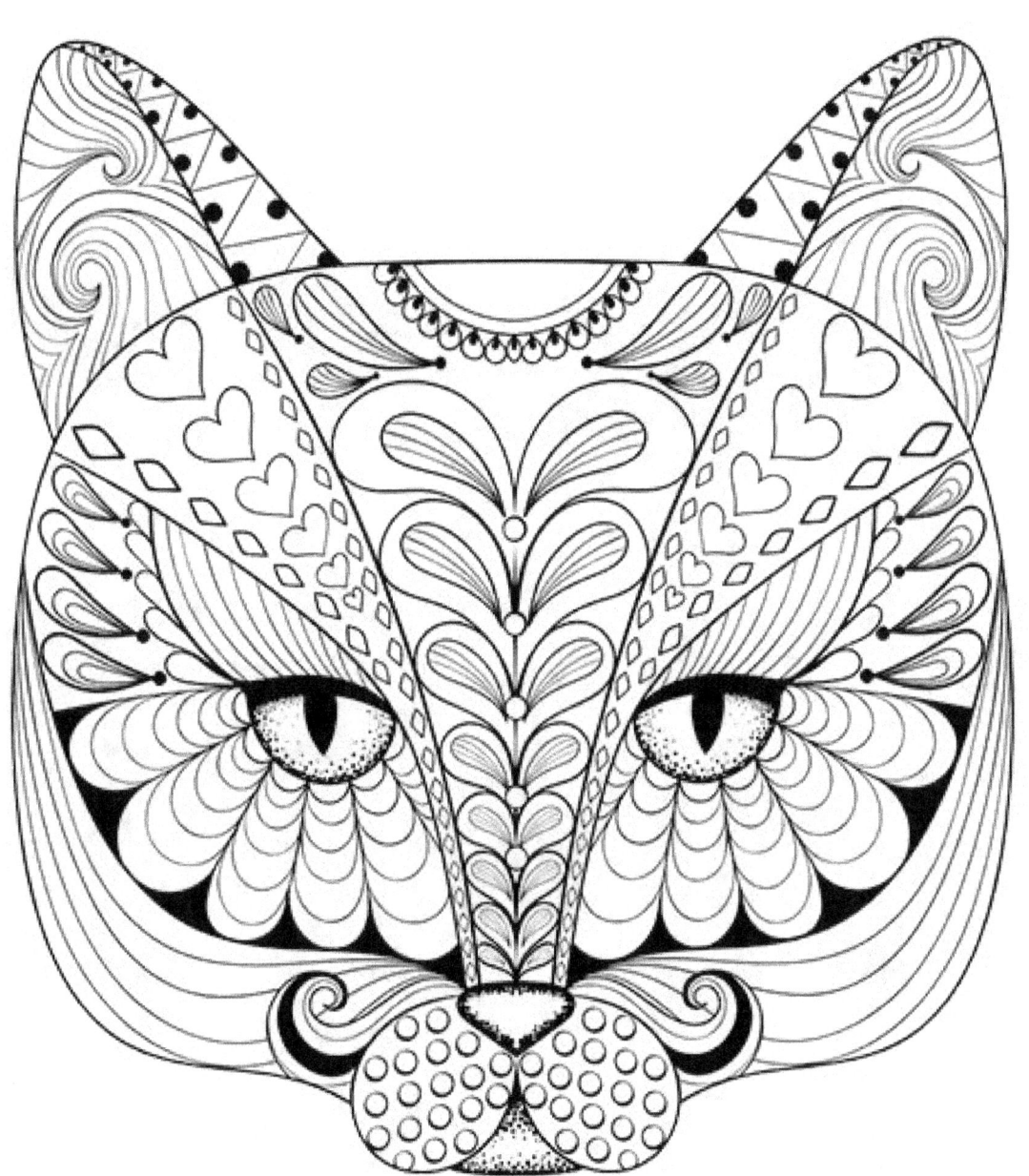

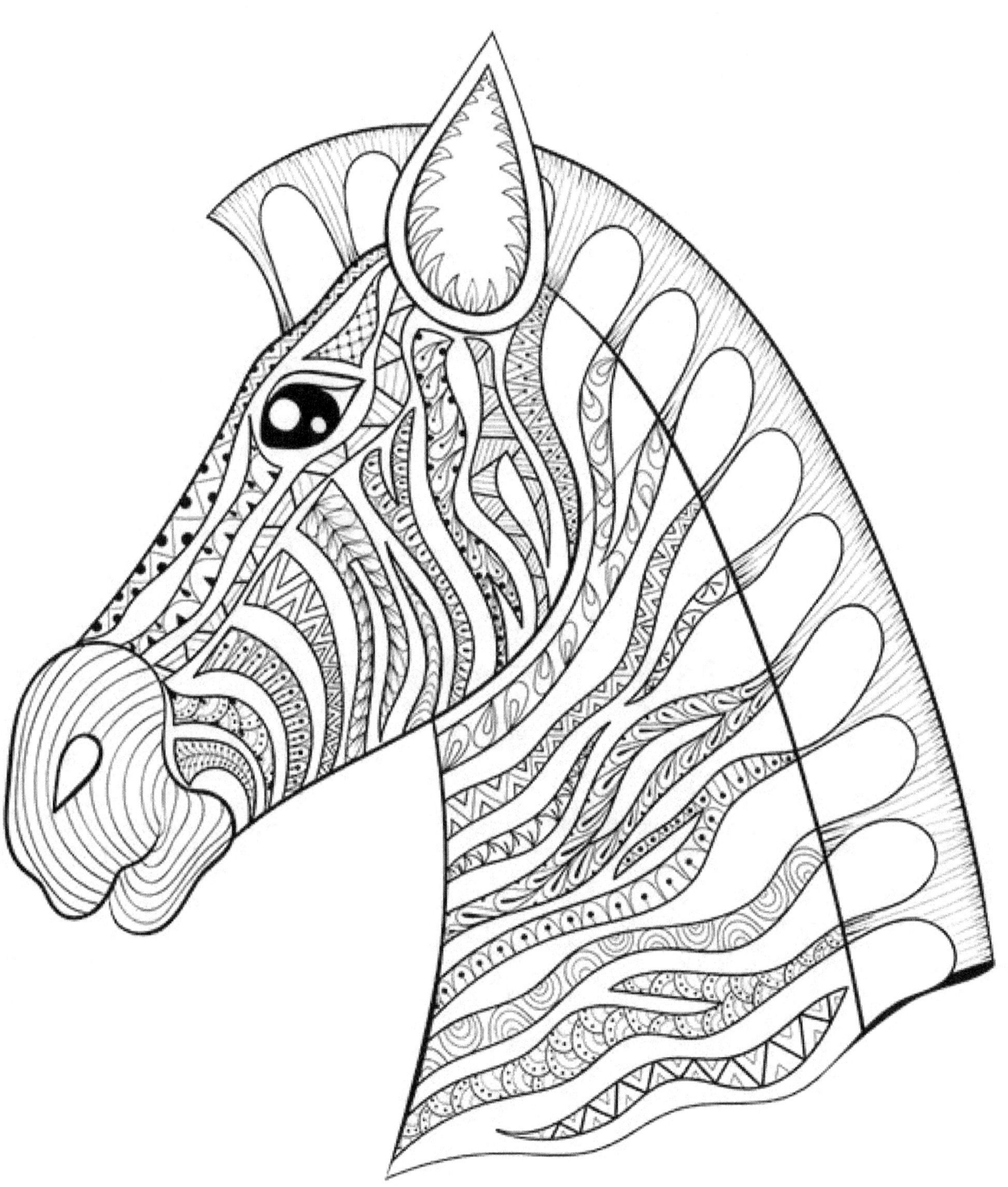

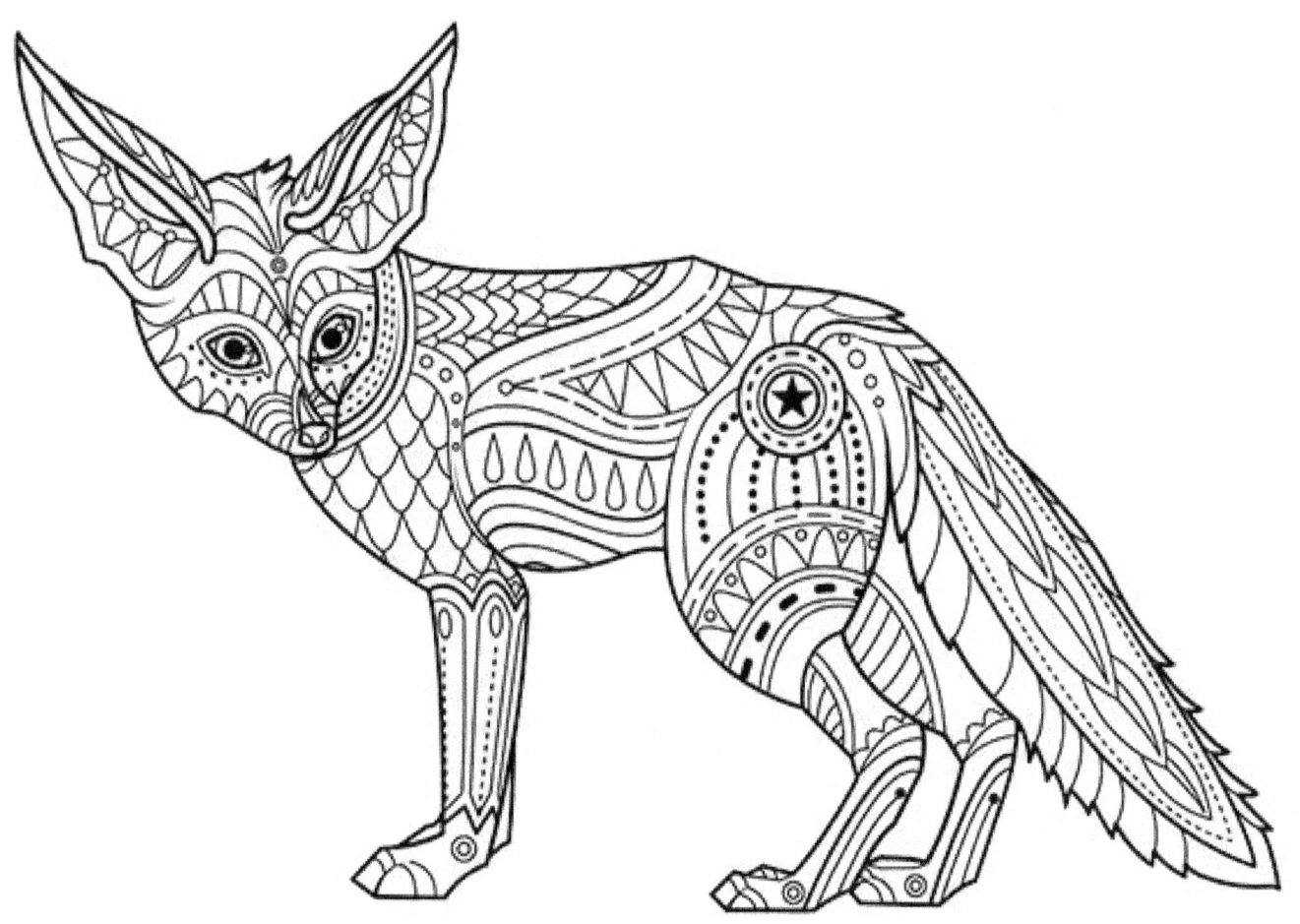

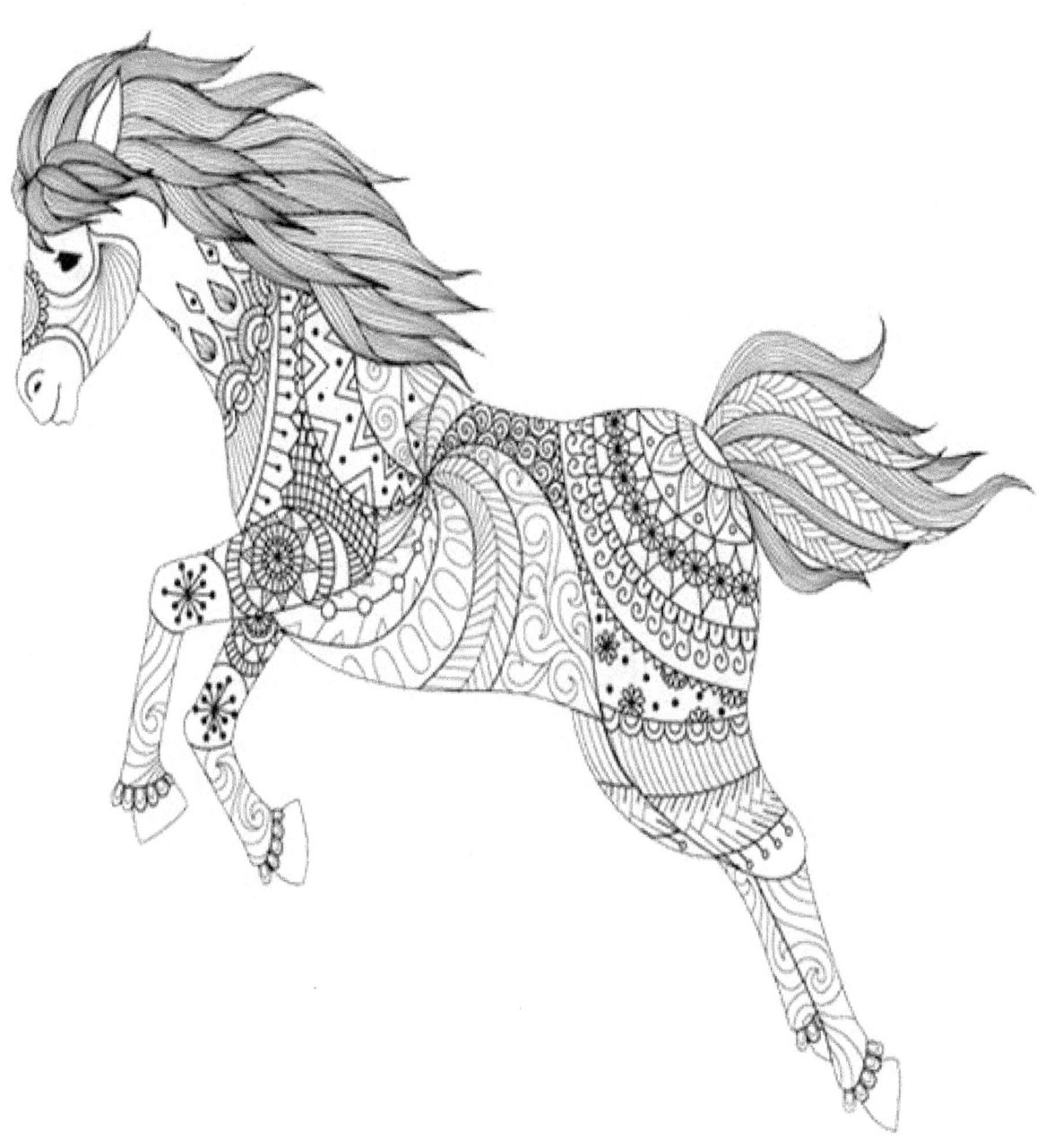

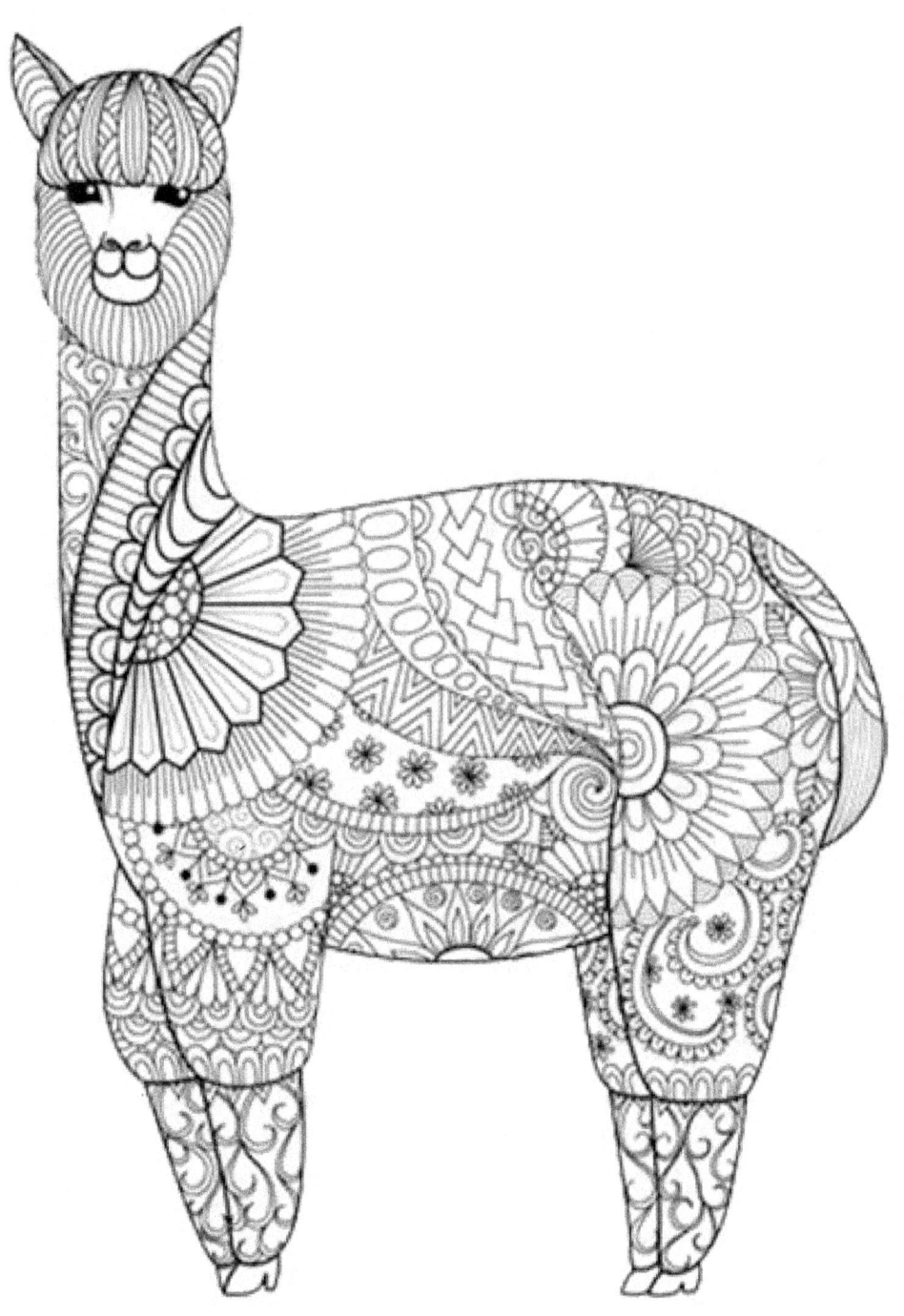

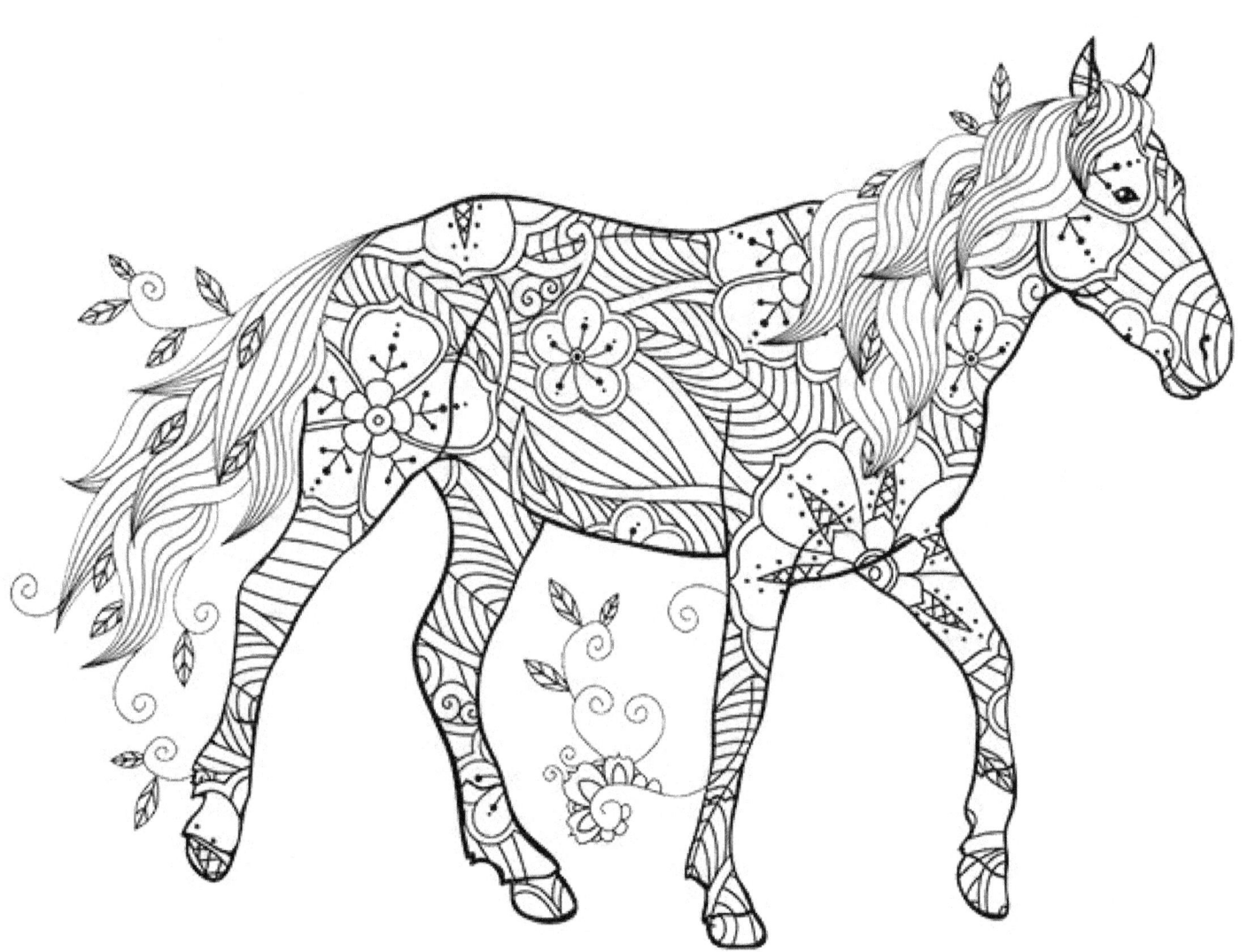

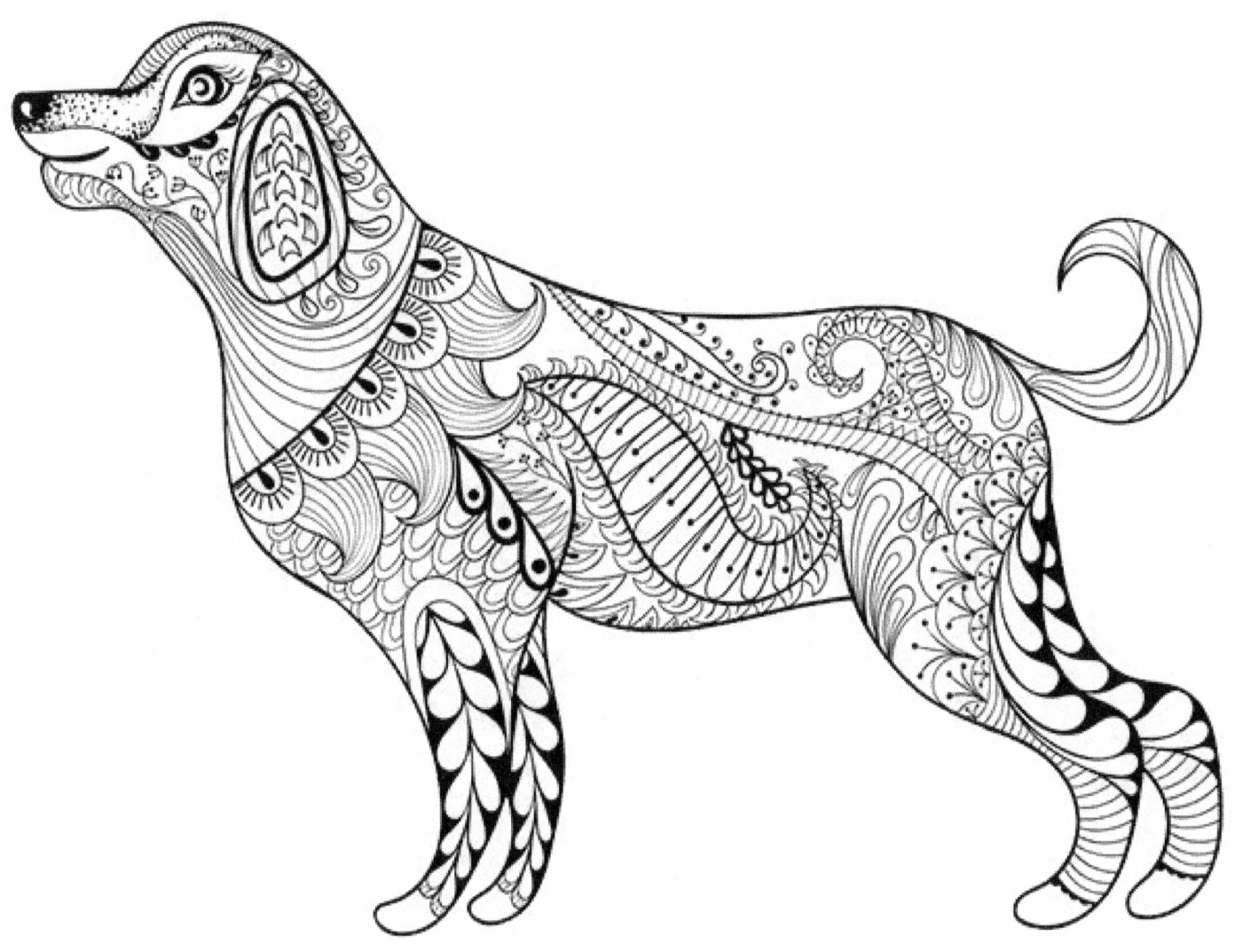

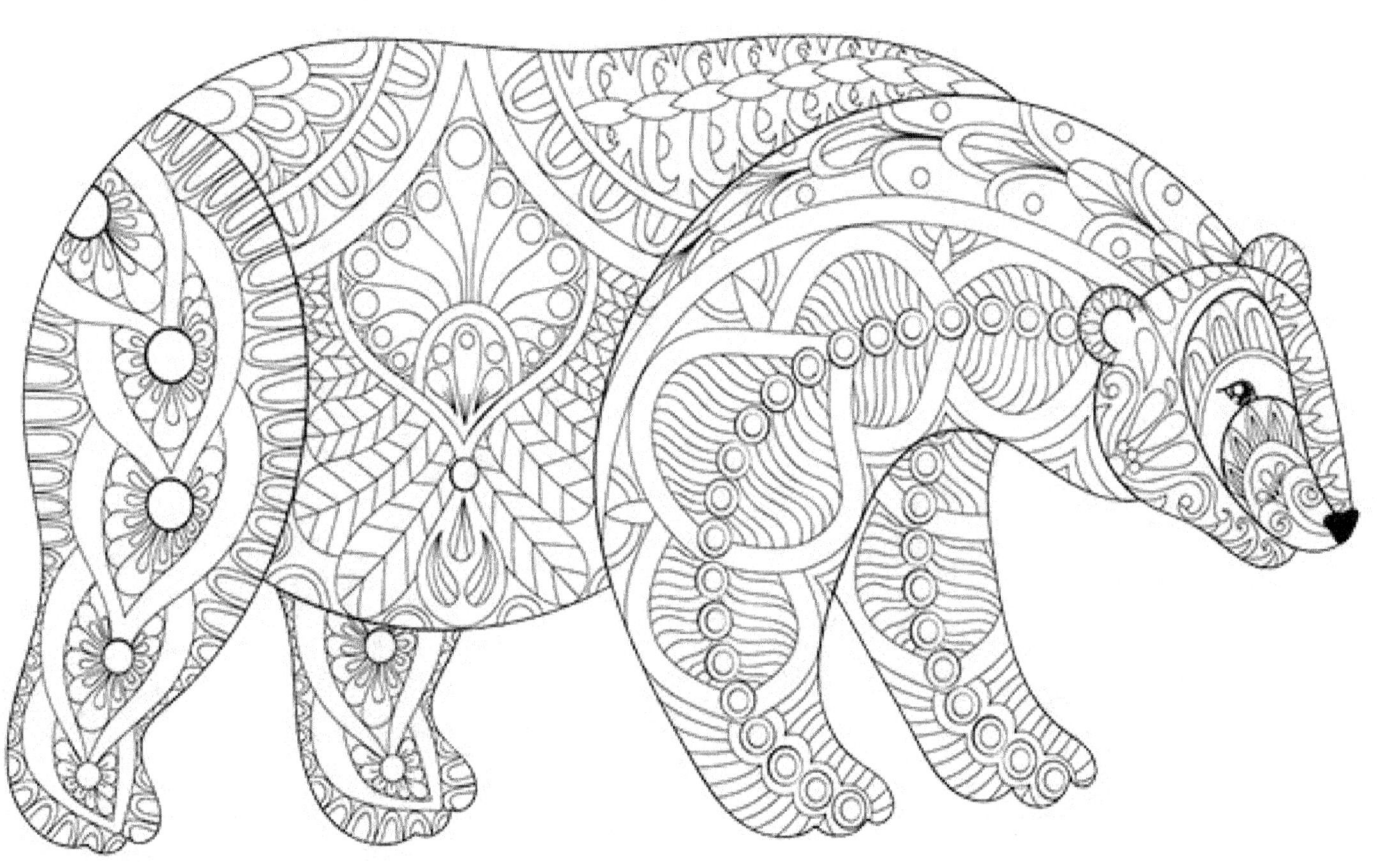

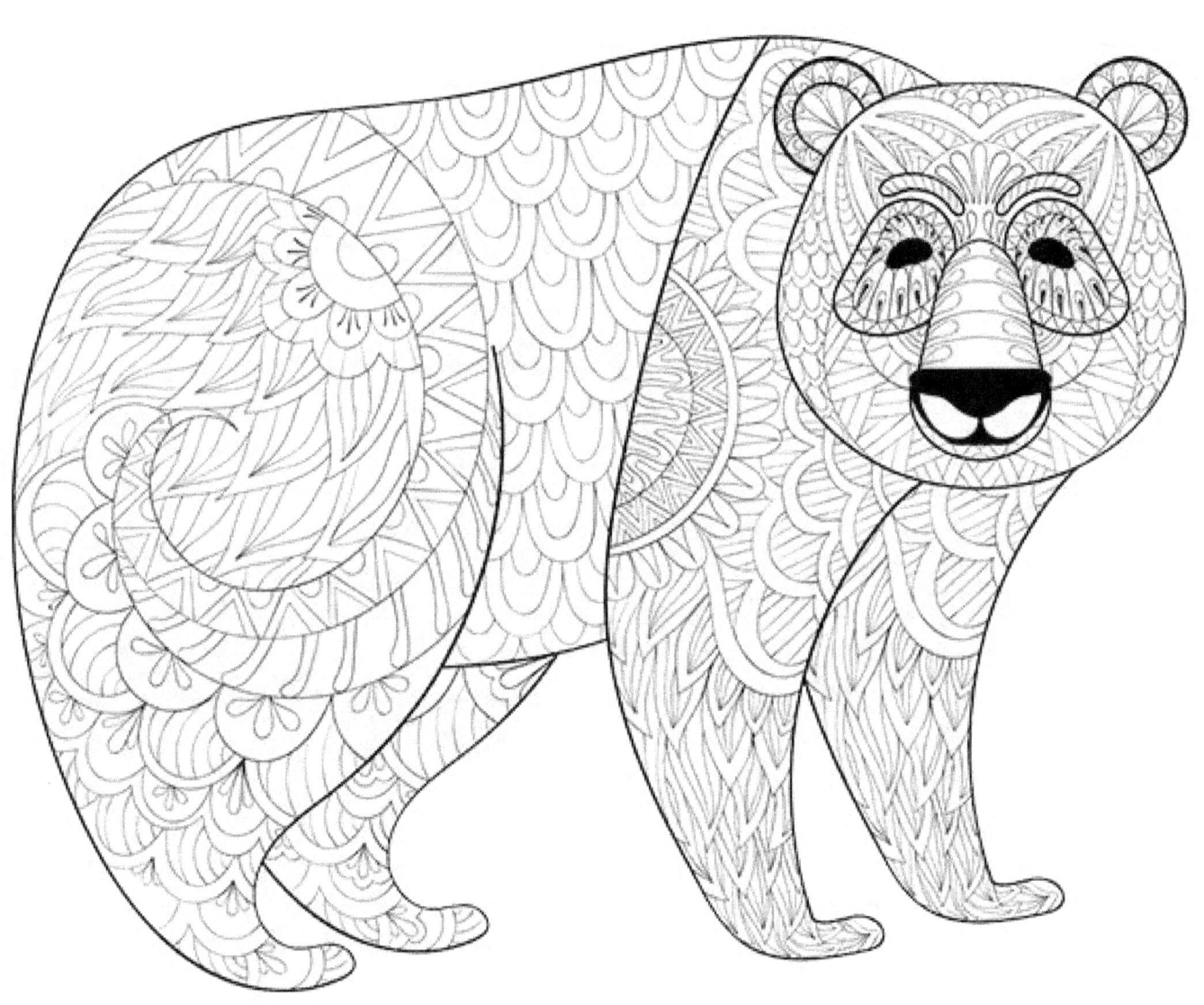

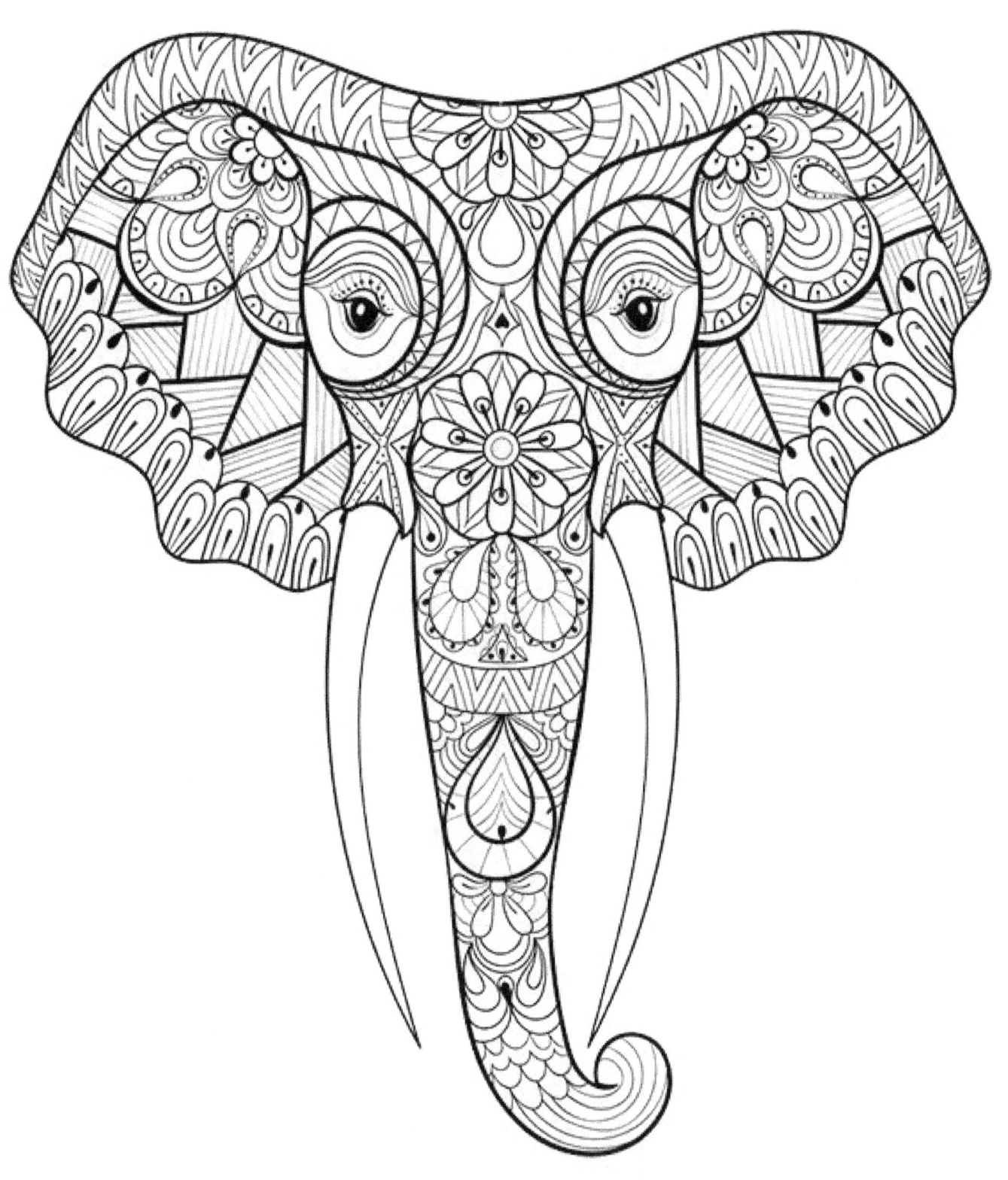

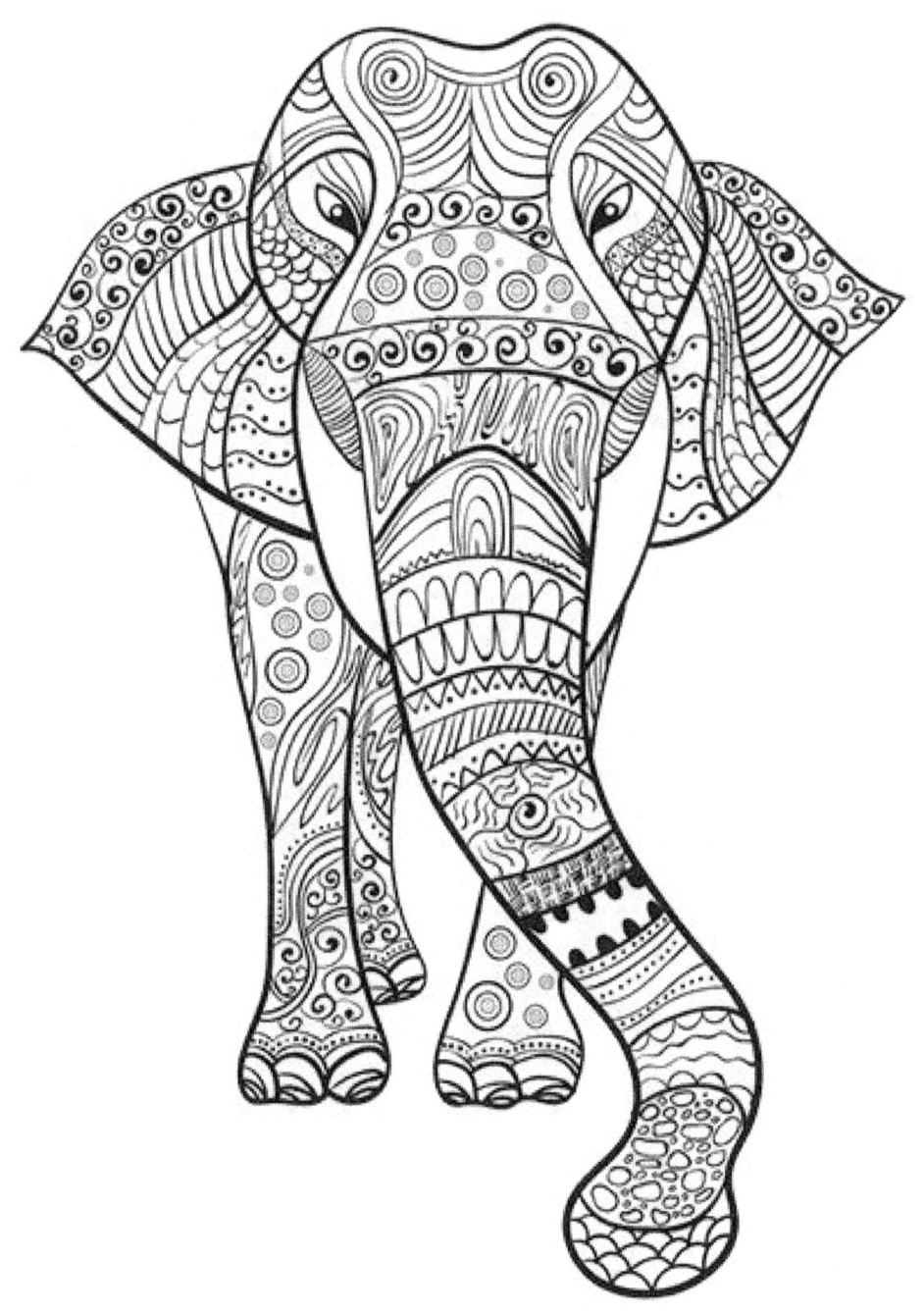

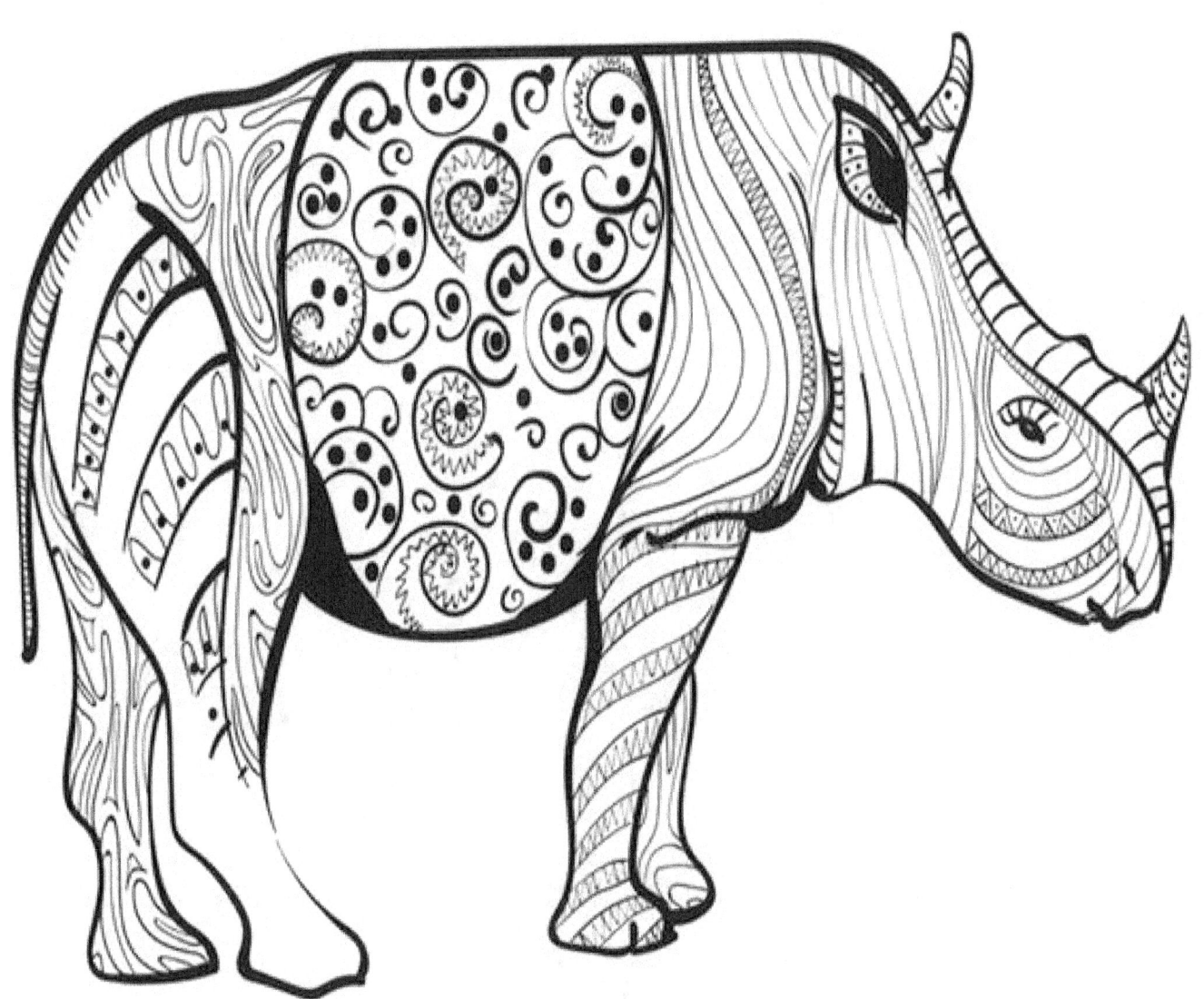

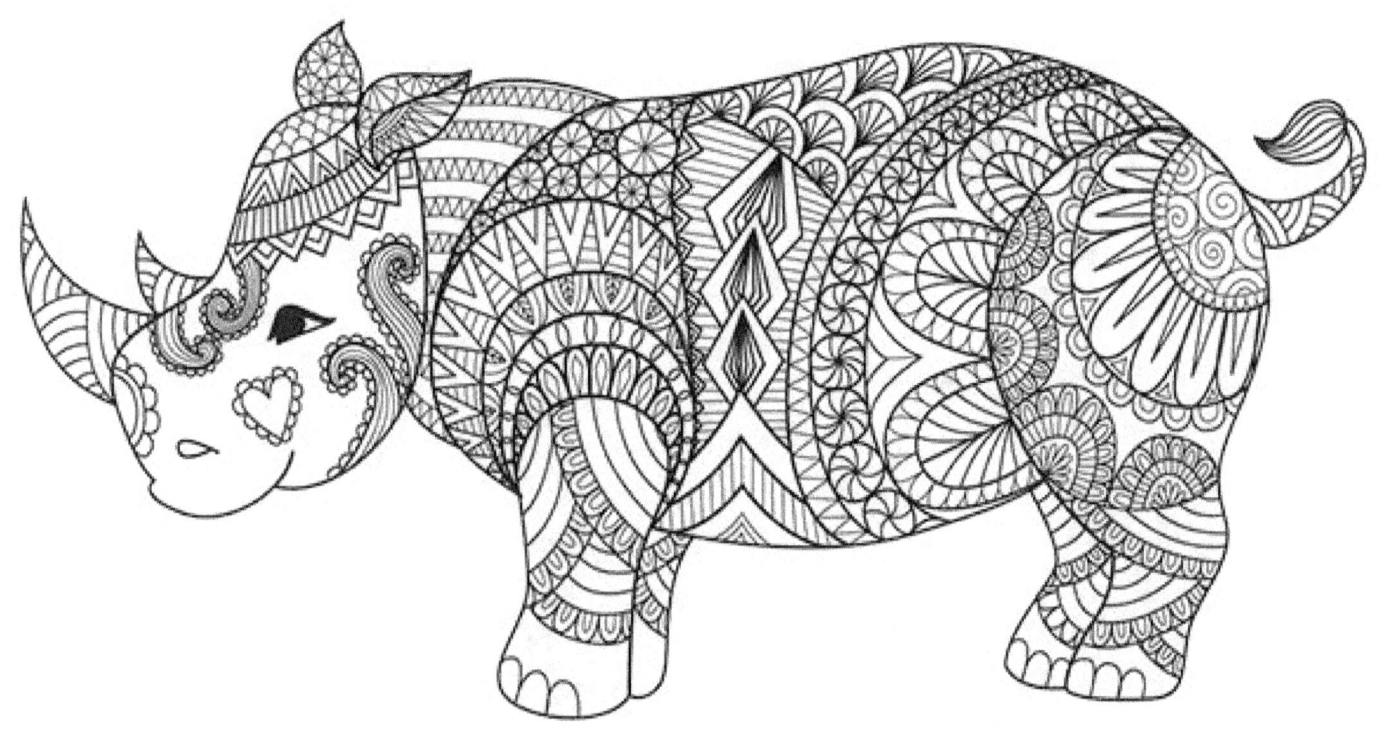

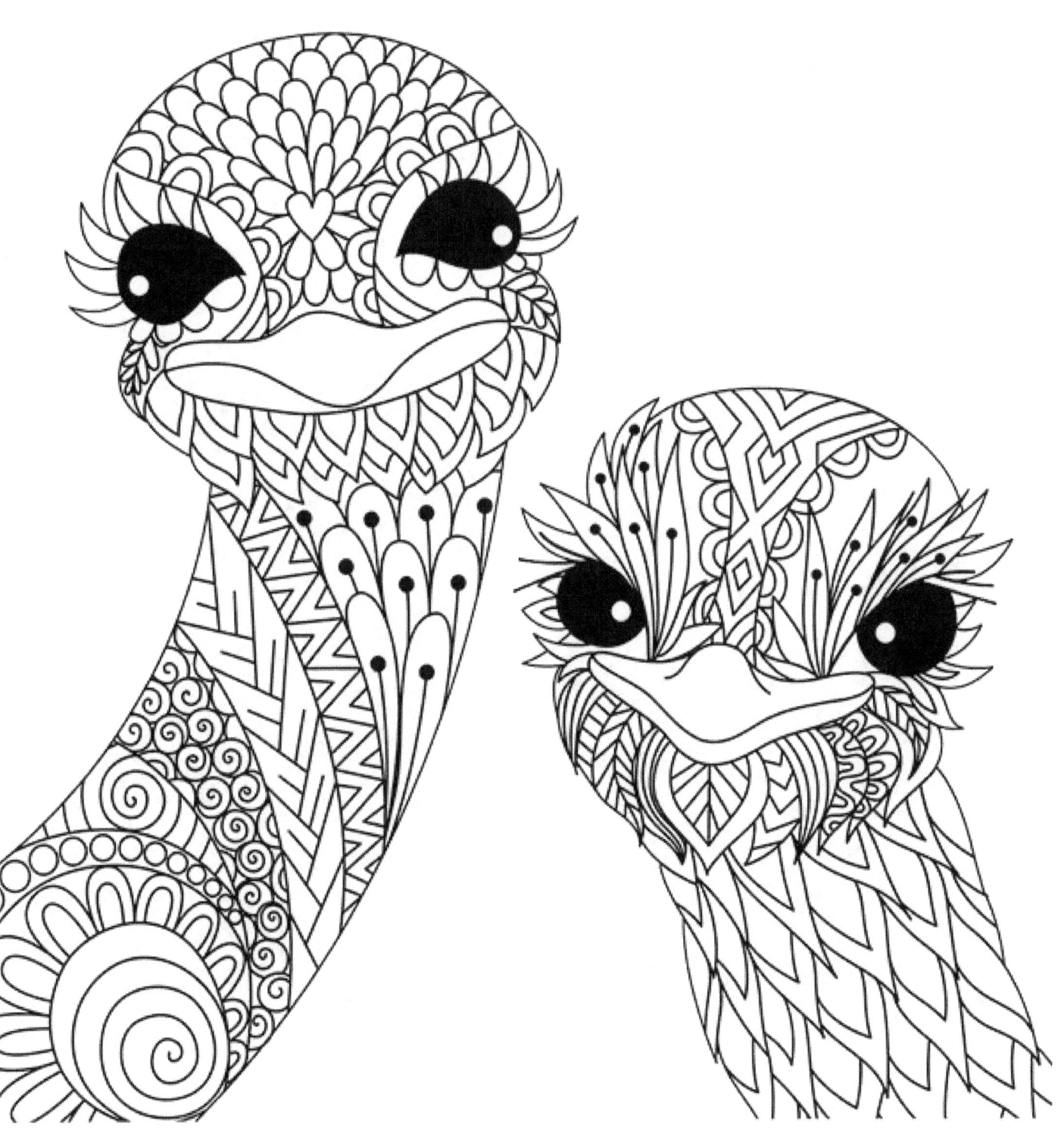

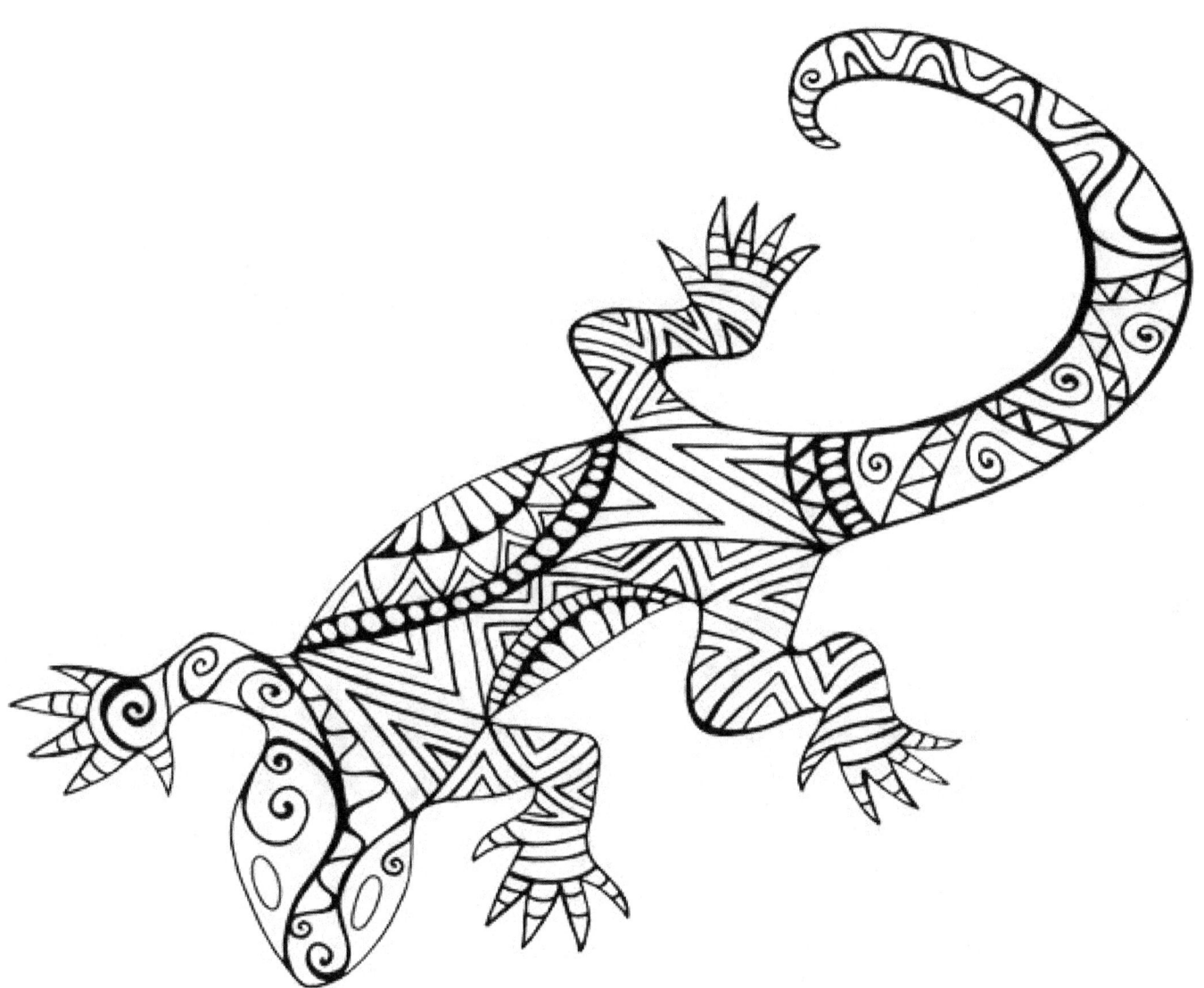

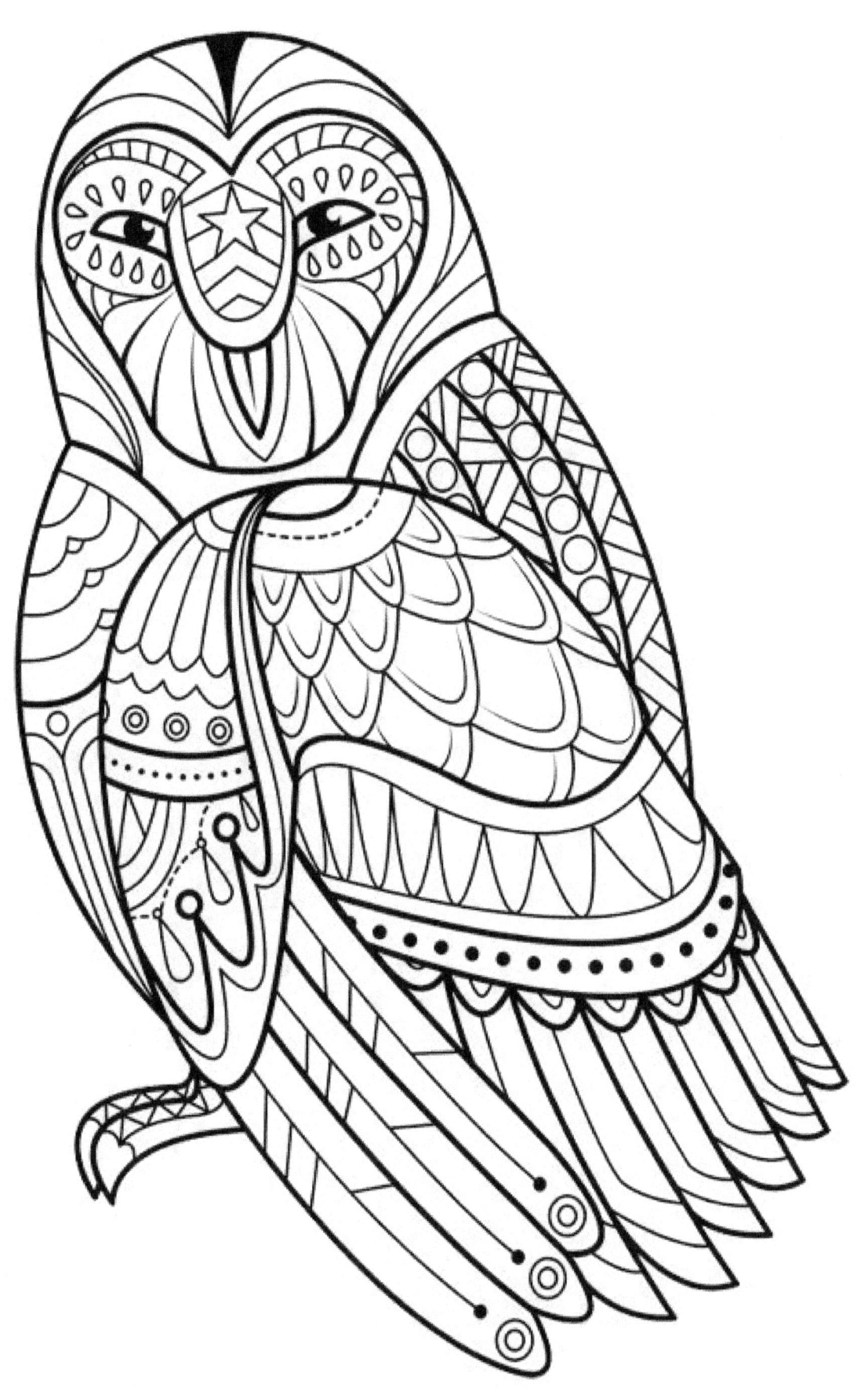

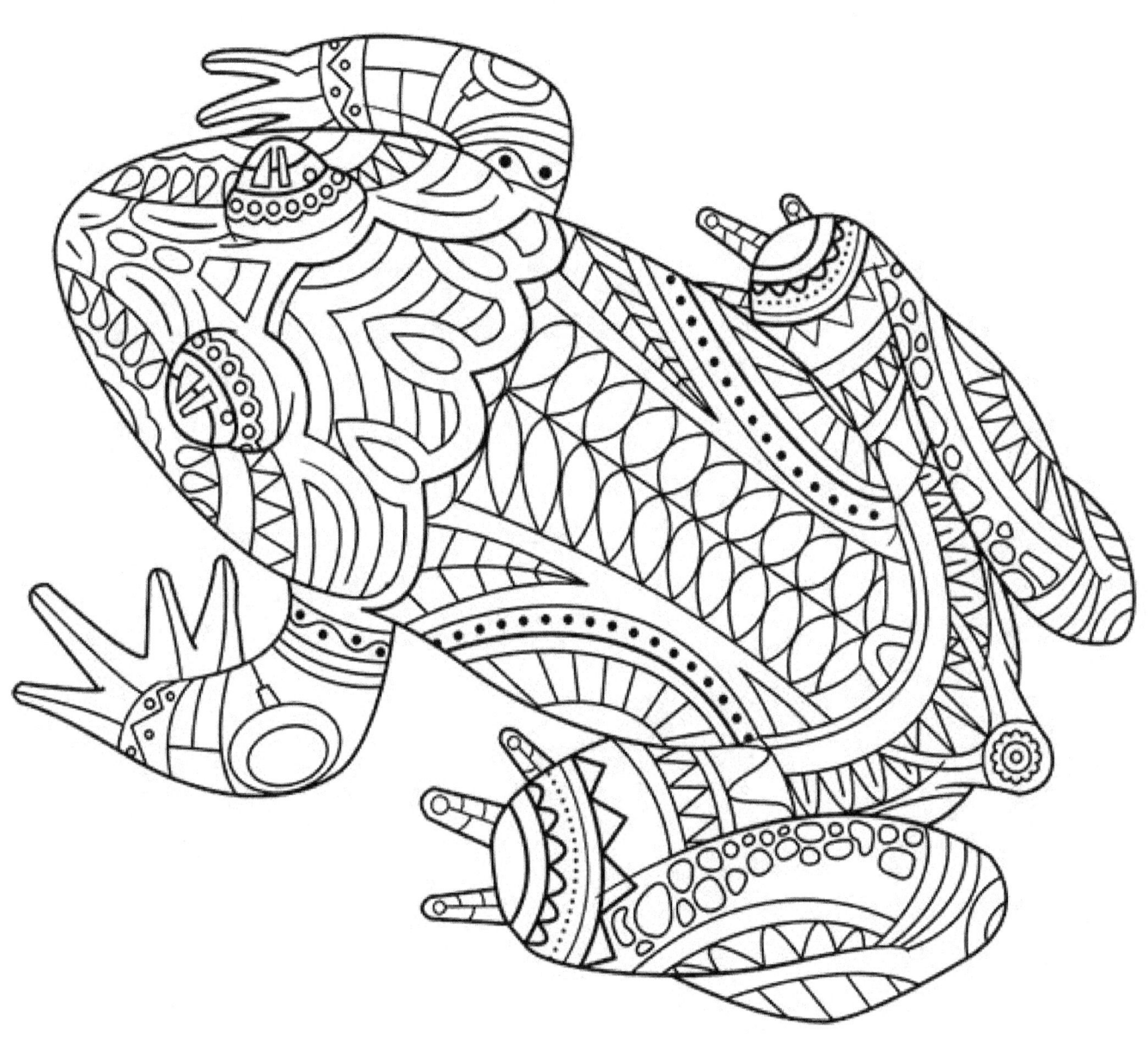

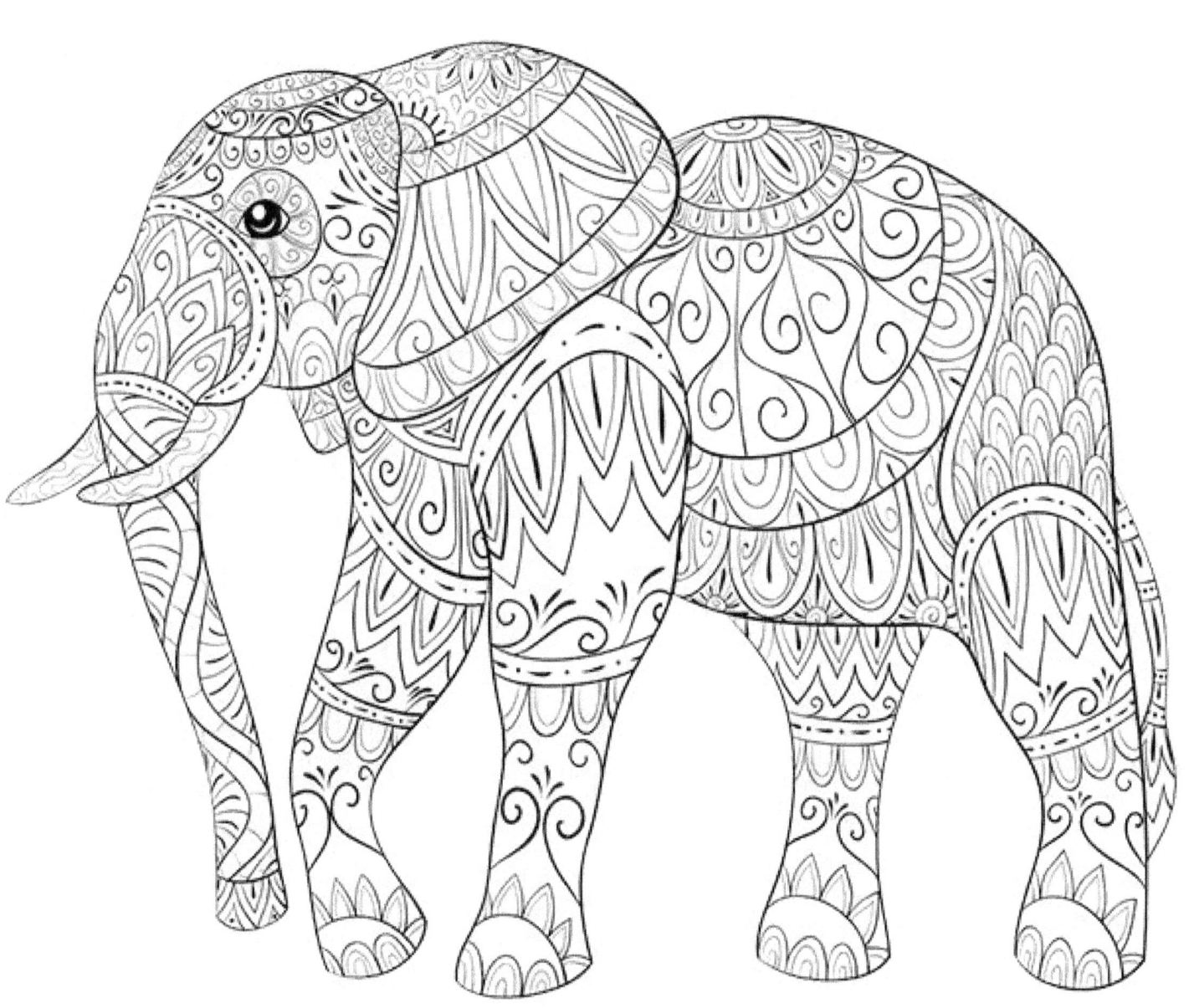

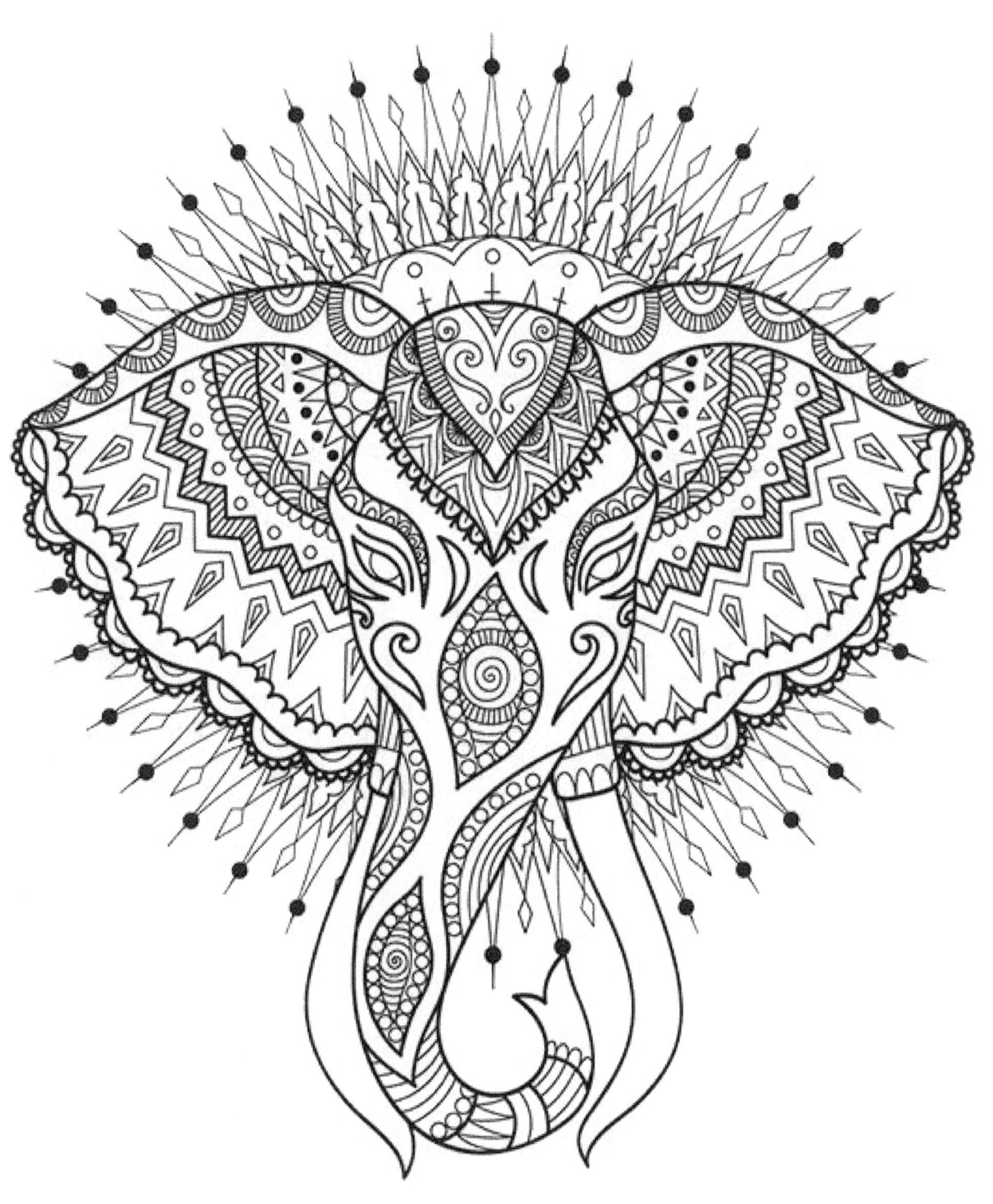

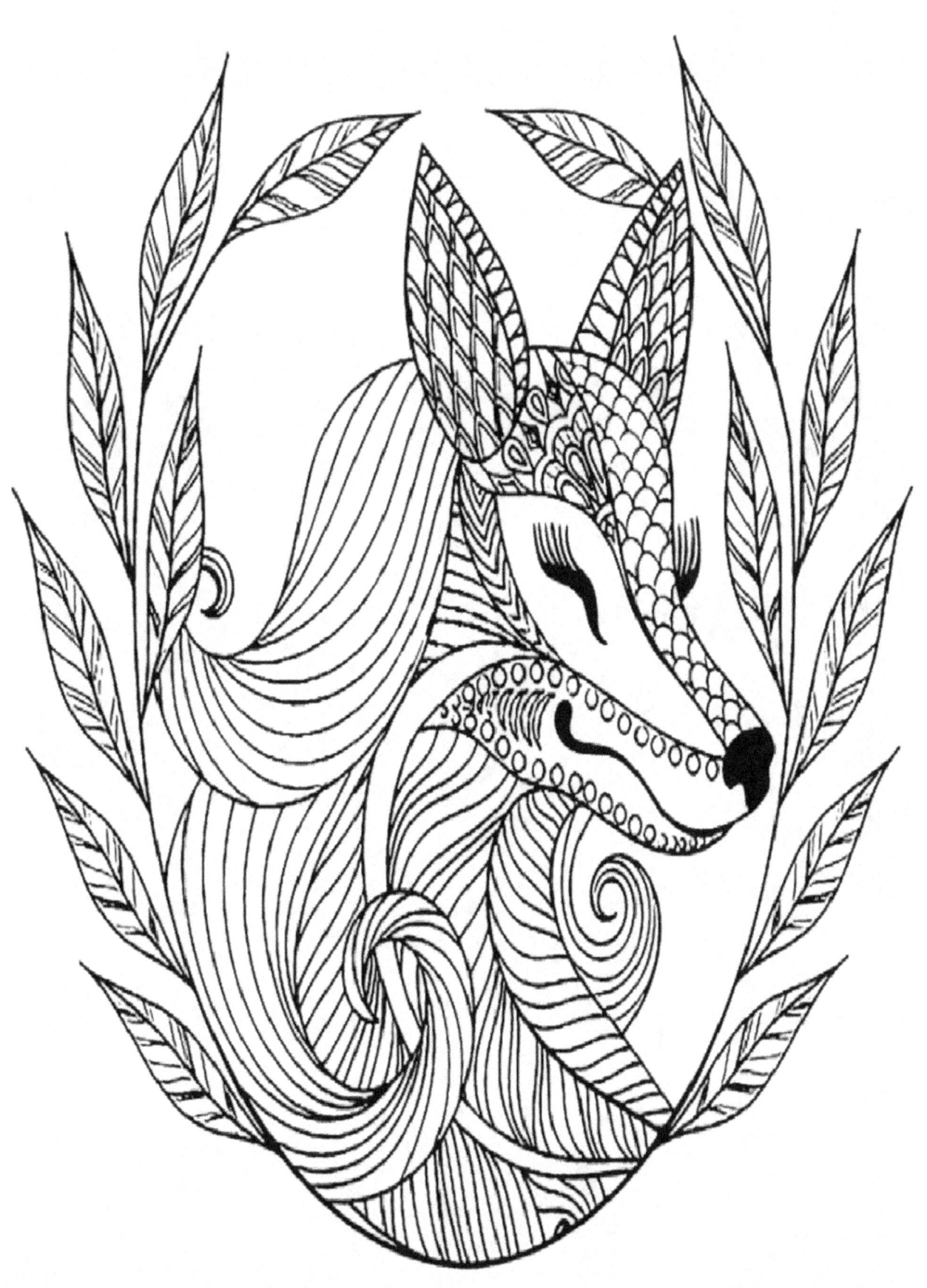

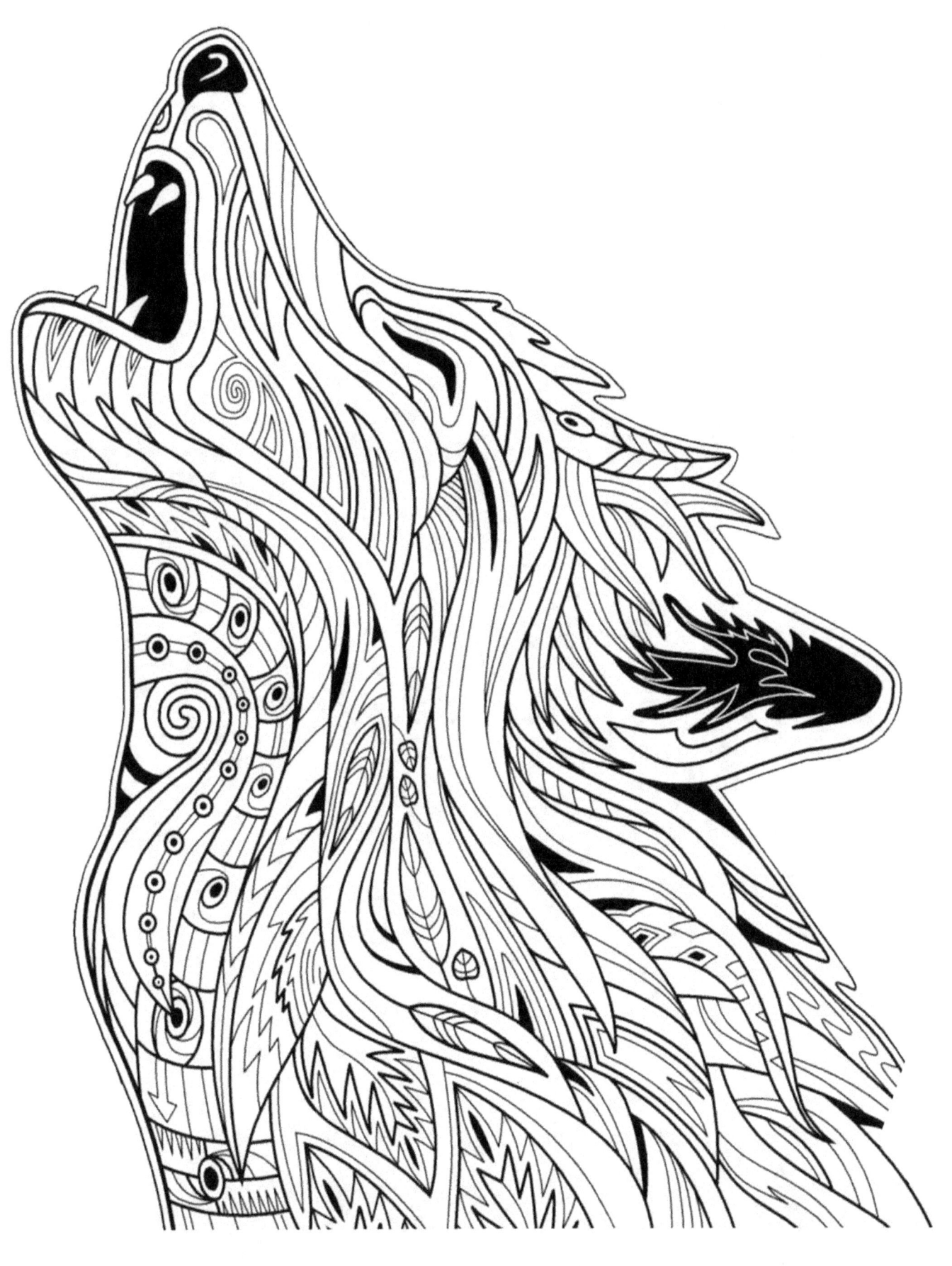

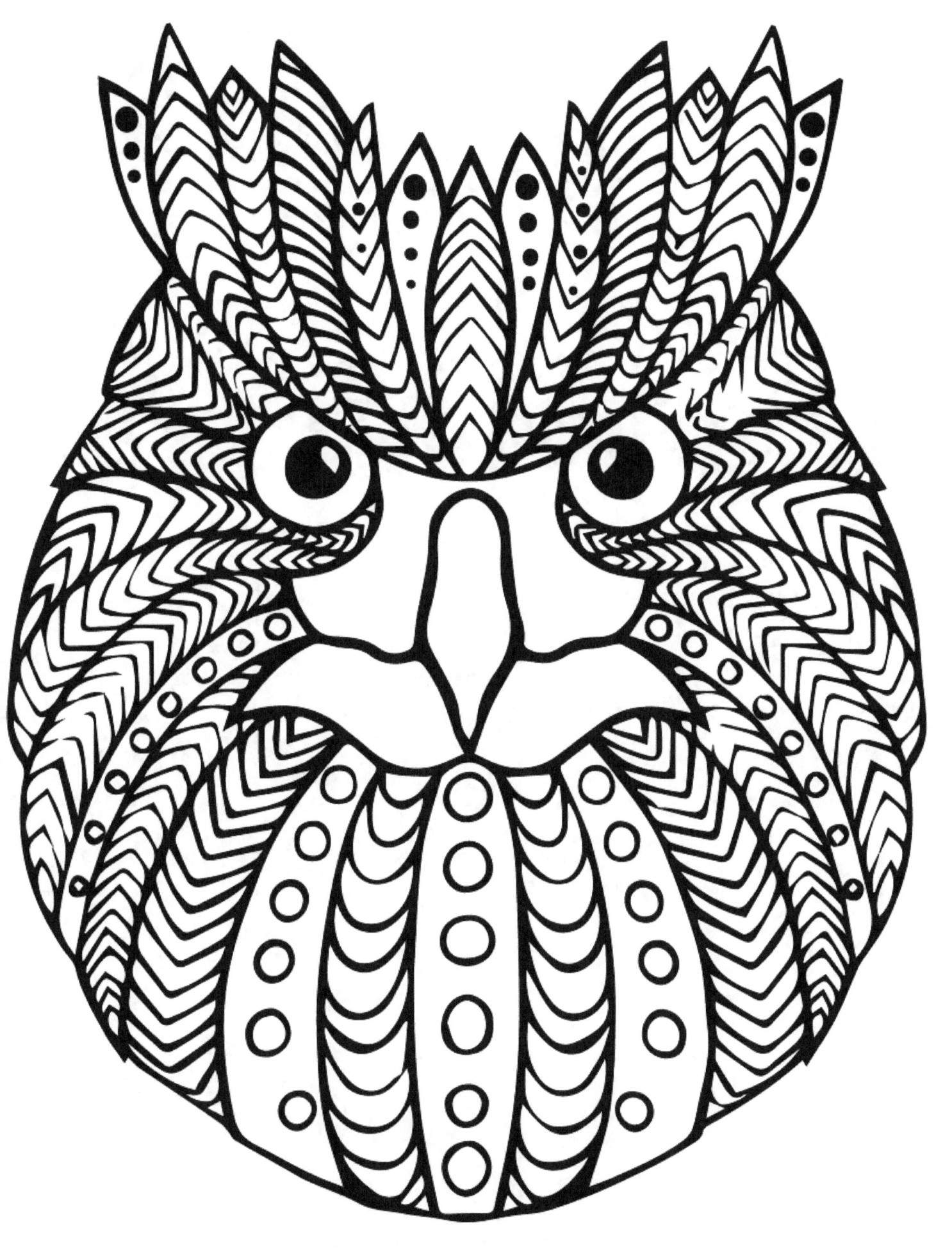

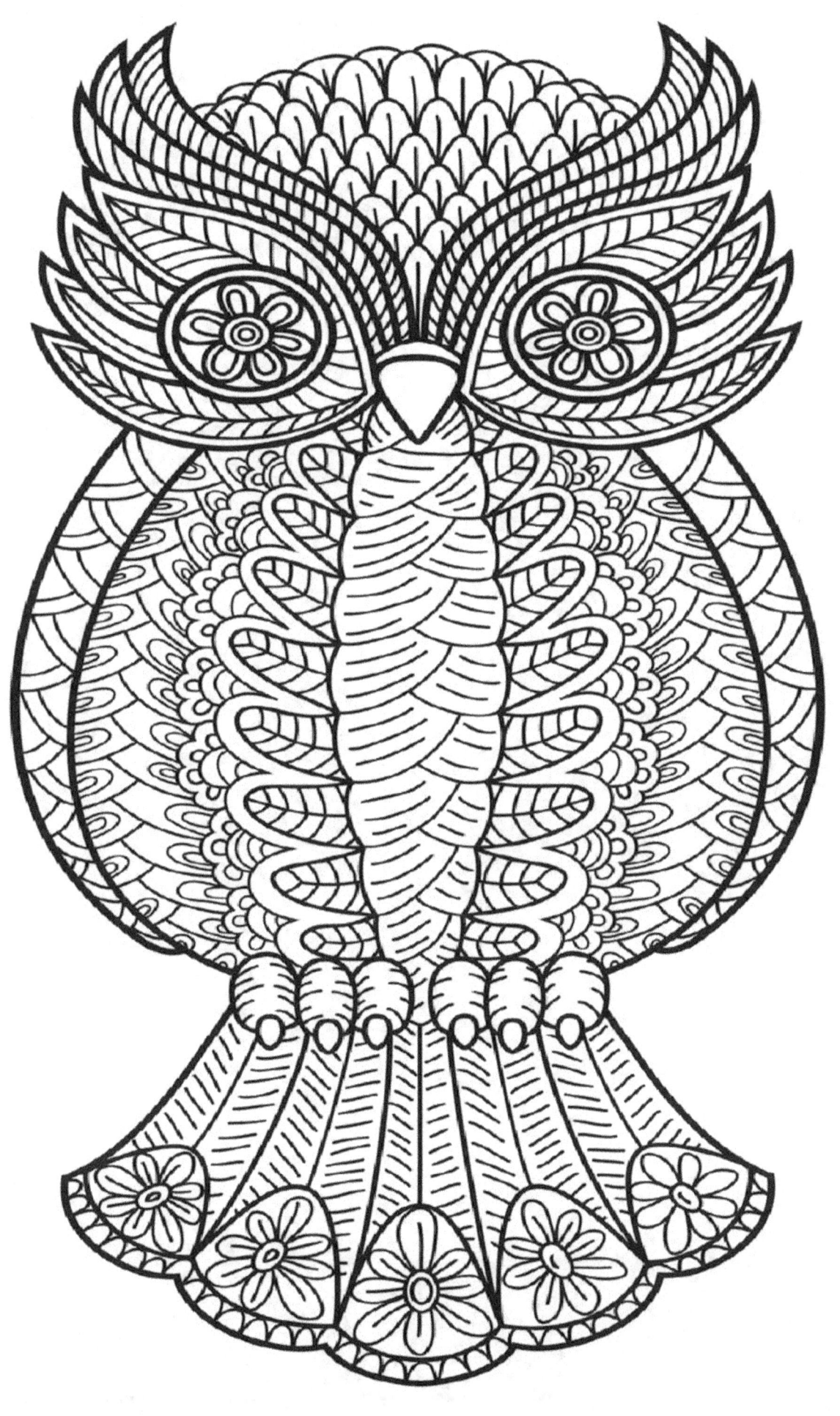

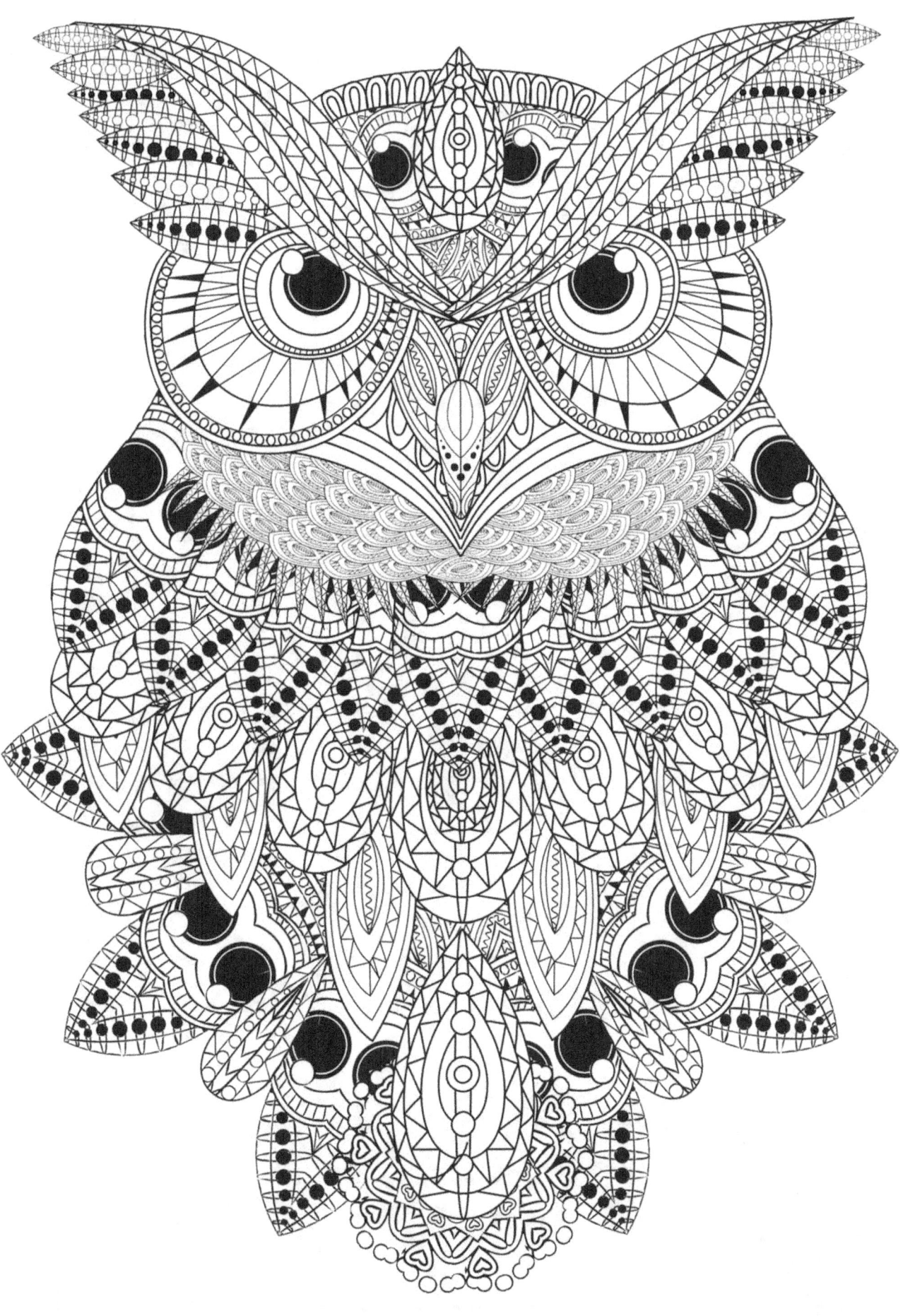

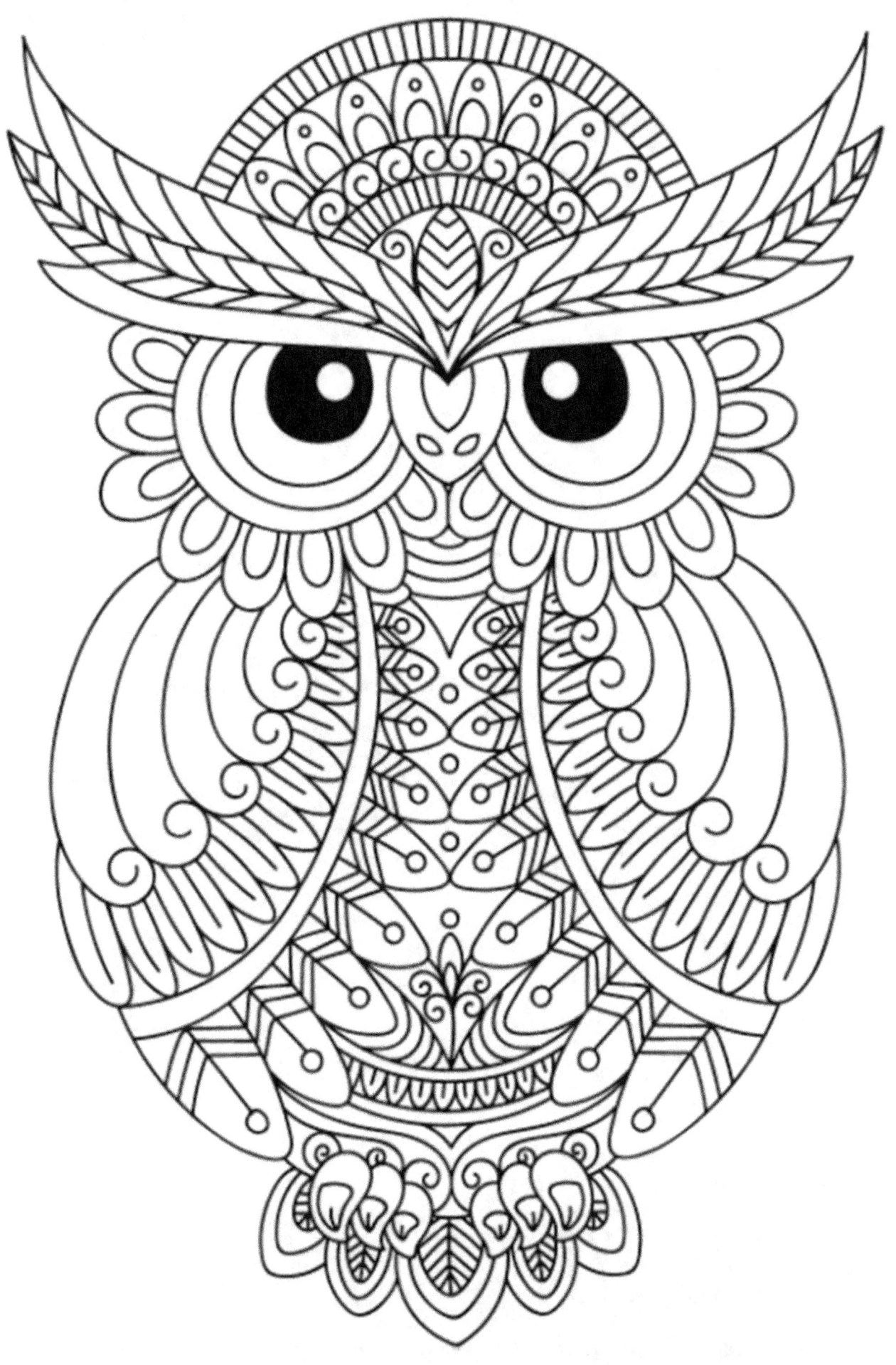

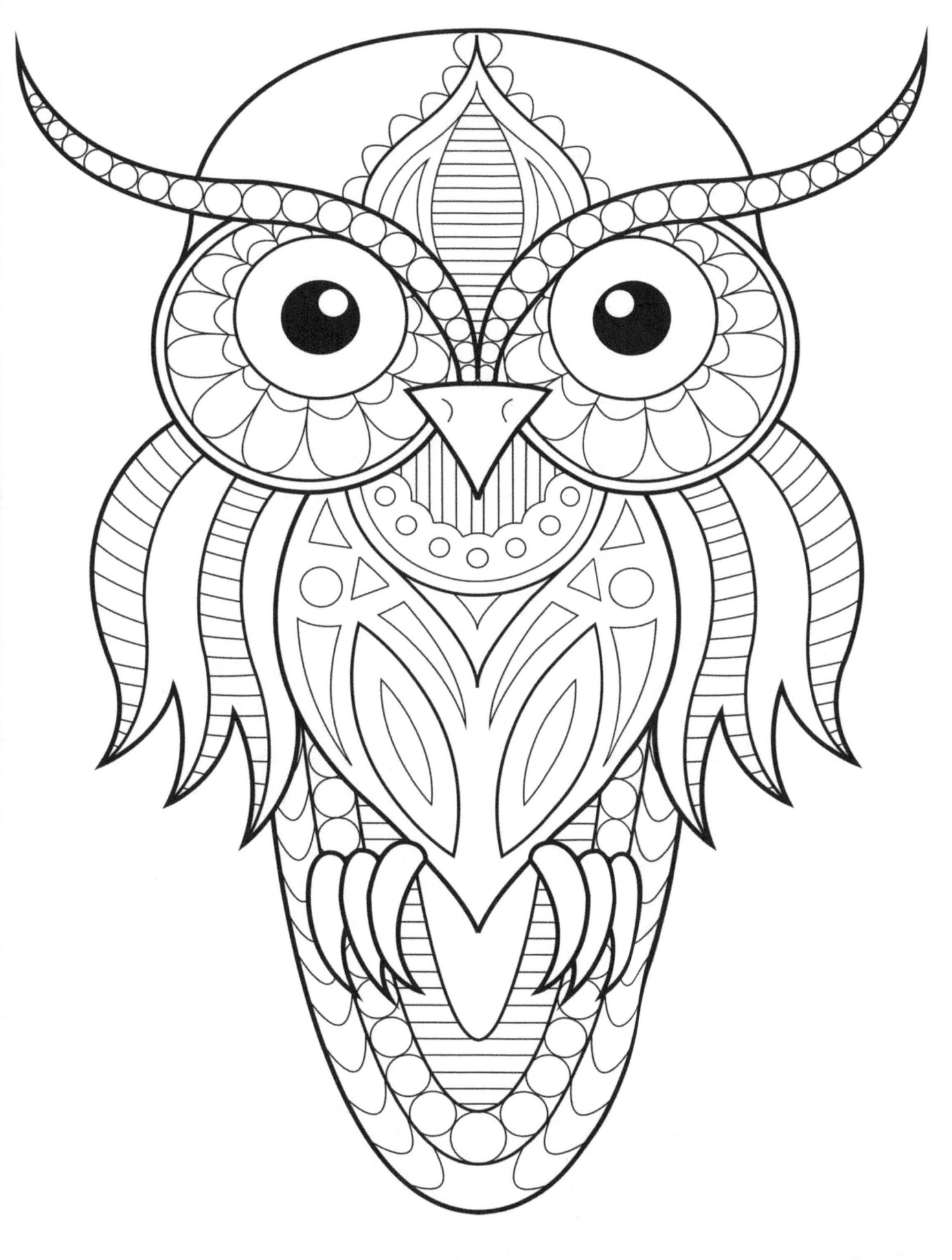

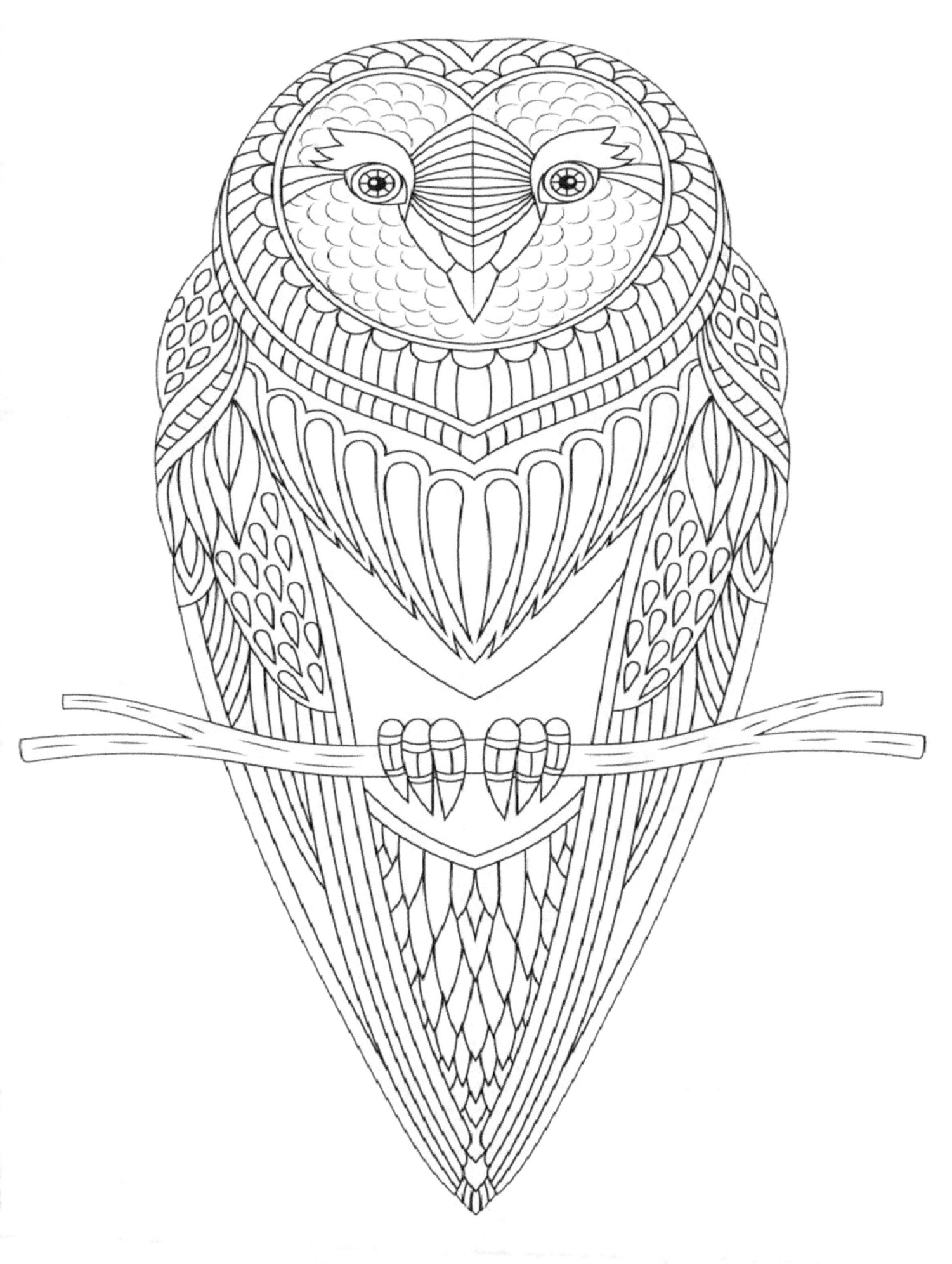

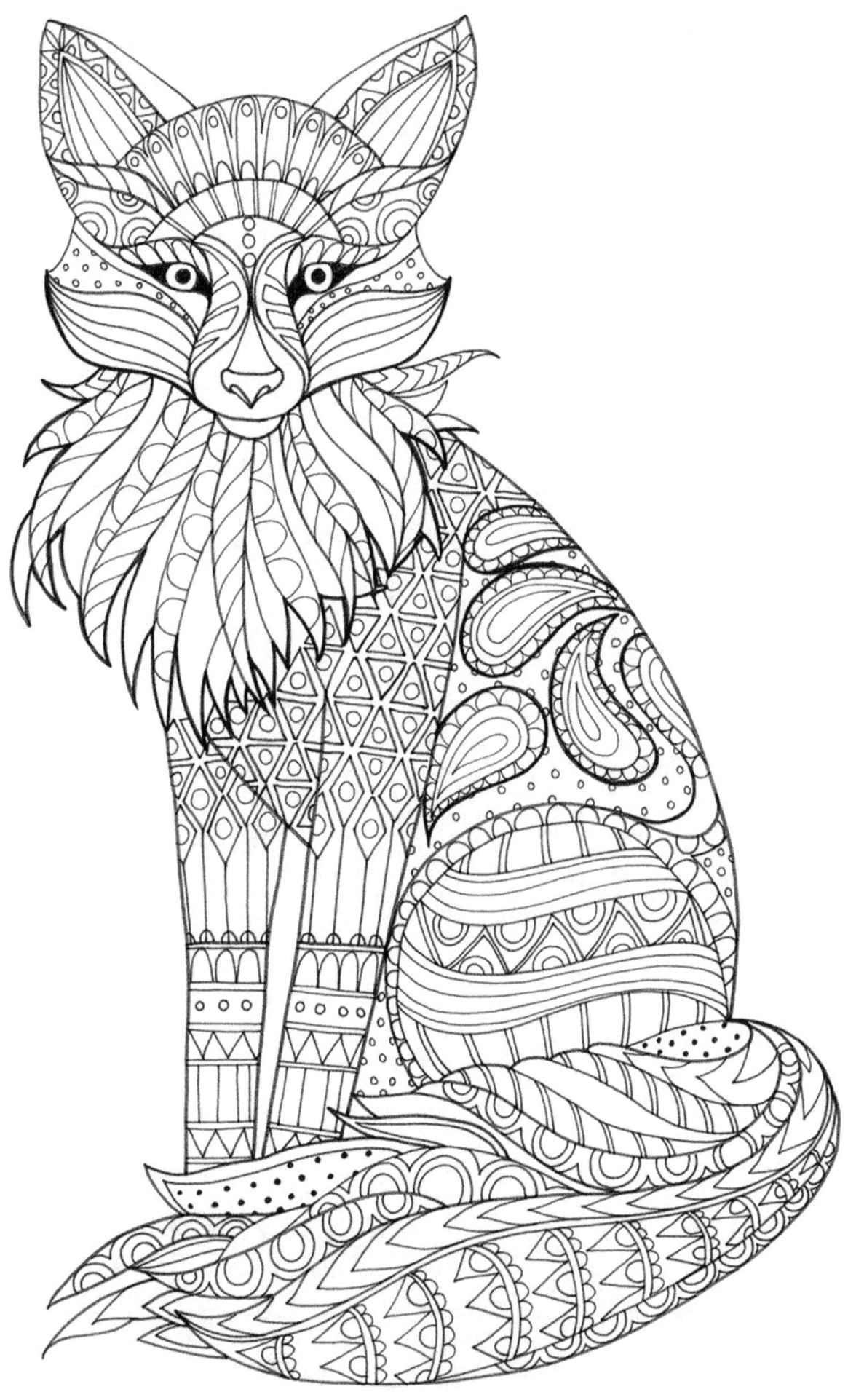

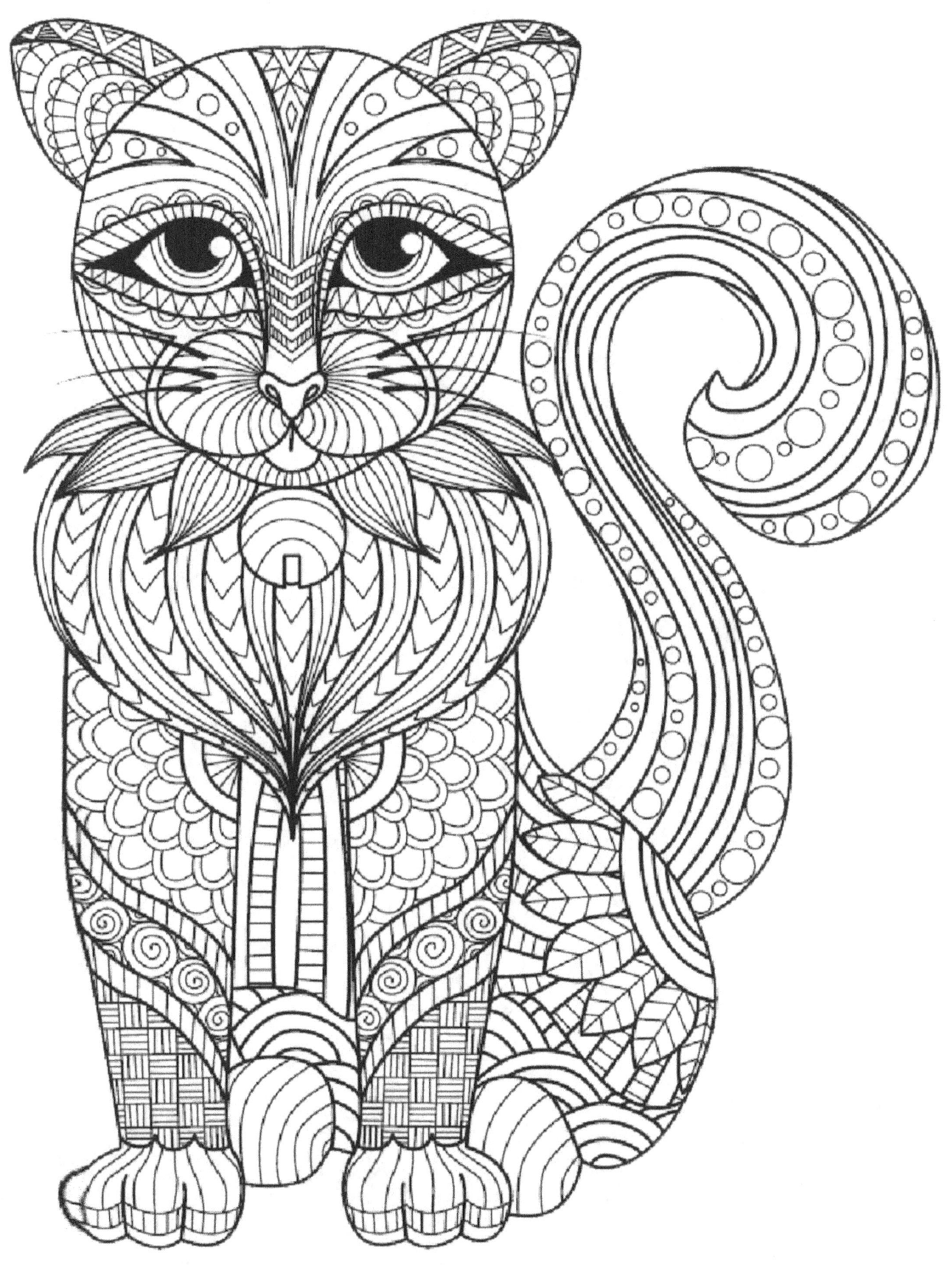

www.ingramcontent.com/pod-product-compliance
Lightning Source LLC
Chambersburg PA
CBHW060426220526

45465CB00008B/3030